Musique Concrète

Forthcoming in the series:

Vaporwave by Kirk Walker Graves
Field Recordings by Marc Weidenbaum
Noise Music by Natalie Marlin
Bollywood by Shwetant Kumar
Neo-Soul by Matthew Allen
Alterlatino by Javier A. Rodríguez-Camacho
Midwest Emo by Will Hagle

Musique Concrète

GENRE
A 33⅓ SERIES

Christian Kriticos

BLOOMSBURY ACADEMIC
NEW YORK • LONDON • OXFORD • NEW DELHI • SYDNEY

BLOOMSBURY ACADEMIC

Bloomsbury Publishing Inc, 1359 Broadway, New York, NY 10018, USA
Bloomsbury Publishing Plc, 50 Bedford Square, London, WC1B 3DP, UK
Bloomsbury Publishing Ireland, 29 Earlsfort Terrace, Dublin 2, D02 AY28, Ireland

BLOOMSBURY, BLOOMSBURY ACADEMIC and the Diana logo are trademarks of Bloomsbury Publishing Plc

First published in the United States of America 2026

Library of Congress Control Number: 2026942163

ISBN: PB:979-8-7651-2332-4
ePDF: 979-8-7651-2334-8
eBook: 979-8-7651-2333-1

Series: 33 1/3 Genre

Typeset by Deanta Global Publishing Services, Chennai, India
Printed and bound in the United States of America

For product safety related questions contact productsafety@bloomsbury.com.

To find out more about our authors and books visit www.bloomsbury.com and sign up for our newsletters.

To Kirsty Archer-Thompson

Contents

Prologue

What on earth is musique concrète?

For most of human history, you could only hear a piece of music once. Whether it was a prehistoric bone flute recital, an Ancient Greek chorus, or the premiere of a Beethoven symphony – each note was like a word written in water, vanishing as soon as it was laid down. But sound is no longer so ephemeral. Recording technologies changed all that. Now, a performer can preserve a definitive recording for listeners to replay in perpetuity.

The earliest pioneers of recording technologies didn't immediately understand this transformative potential. In fact, the very first recording device, the phonautograph, was not even able to play the audio back! Created in 1857 by French inventor Édouard-Léon Scott de Martinville, the machine simply inscribed sound waves on paper.[1] It would be another 20 years before Thomas Edison's similarly named phonograph became the first machine to both record *and* reproduce sound. Using the same principles as Scott's device, it inscribed sound waves on a cylinder wrapped in foil. By tracing a stylus

---

[1] Jody Rosen, 'Researchers Play Tune Recorded Before Edison', *New York Times*, 27 March 2008, https://www.nytimes.com/2008/03/27/arts/27soun.html.

back through these grooves, the sound vibrations could be replicated and amplified.[2]

Eventually, discs superseded Edison's cylinders. These were easier to transport, store and play. But their recording technique still followed the same principle, using gigantic horns to receive sound waves acoustically. The next breakthrough came when electronics entered the scene. Using microphones, audio could now be converted into an electronic signal as it was recorded. The first recording technology to be activated electrically was the wire recorder. This device worked by pulling a length of thin steel wire between two spools. As it moved across the recording head, the wire would be magnetized to capture the sound being received. That principle would later give rise to tape recorders, which similarly magnetized a metal or plastic ribbon as it moved between two spools. Tape made audio editing much easier and allowed for many new innovations, including multitracking, in which different sounds are held on separate 'channels' on the same piece of tape.[3]

Despite the gradual improvements among these early recording technologies, they all ultimately allowed for the same groundbreaking purpose – the transcription of a musical performance from time to space. While music was previously fated to die an immediate death on the winds of time, recording technologies enabled it to be made physical – carved into the

---

[2]'History of the Cylinder Phonograph', Library of Congress, https://www.loc.gov/collections/edison-company-motion-pictures-and-sound-recordings/articles-and-essays/history-of-edison-sound-recordings/history-of-the-cylinder-phonograph/.

[3]Thom Holmes, *Electronic and Experimental Music: Technology, Music, and Culture* sixth edition (New York: Routledge, 2020), 189.

spiralized pathways of a gramophone disc, or encoded into a length of magnetized wire or tape. For the first time in history, these technologies allowed a musical performance to be held in human hands. And with the ability to physically grasp a moment of time also came the opportunity to manipulate that time and unlock new sounds never heard by earthly ears.

In the case of a phonograph disc, one could speed up or slow down the playback to alter the pitch. With wire, one could cut and weld sections together, enabling instantaneous jumps between separate moments in time. And, with magnetic tape, one could run the audio backwards, creating strange effects that would be impossible to reproduce organically.

These techniques revealed that every sound contains multitudes. And once you can hold a piece of sound in your hands, you have the power to unlock those hidden multitudes – to find the sound within the sound. One genre, known as musique concrète (concrete music), took this idea as its central credo. It determined that the infinity of sound made available by recording technologies meant that music no longer needed to be bound by conventional instruments or the human voice. The recording technology itself could become the instrument.

Thus, musique concrète took recorded sound as its source material. That could be anything: trundling trains, clattering saucepans, or the noise of human laughter. Using turntables, wire recorders and tape machines, musique concrète practitioners played with these sounds as you might play with pieces of clay – warping and shaping them to find those new noises hidden within. Finally, they would assemble their strange sounds into abstract audio collages, unbound by musical conventions such as meter or melody.

Pierre Schaeffer, the father of the genre, felt unsure if this new artistic form could even be defined as music. '[T]he recording of sound is about to upset music,' he announced. 'Something new is added: a new art of sound. Am I wrong in still calling it music?'[4] Indeed, Schaeffer's name for his genre seemed to embody that uncertainty – because how can something as ethereal as music be as solid as concrete?

But that strange contradiction also got to the heart of what musique concrète was trying to do. Because while traditional music is malleable, musique concrète is fixed. An ordinary song might be recorded in the studio, but its music can still be notated and performed live or reinterpreted by anyone. Musique concrète is different. There is no defined way to represent its sound on a musical score. And there is no way to recreate it with instruments in a live setting. For the concrete composer, the sounds are mixed and poured through the recording technology of their choice and, once set, the resulting piece is as fixed and immovable as concrete – forever.

In this way, musique concrète represented a rebellion against the conventions of musical performance, with a gesture towards immortality. In some ways, the genre succeeded in that lofty aim. But, fittingly for the hubris of its ambition, that success came with a cruel twist: as far as most people today are concerned, musique concrète is a dead genre, with vanishingly few practitioners and almost no listeners. Instead, its immortality comes through its myriad influences

[4]Otto Luening, 'Origins', in *The Development and Practice of Electronic Music*, ed. Jon H. Appleton and Ronald C. Perera (Englewood Cliffs: Prentice-Hall Inc., 1975), 11.

on other genres, which can still be heard everywhere: from the sampling technique of hip-hop to the babbling brook on your yoga instructor's favourite meditation playlist.

So, that name – musique concrète – becomes appropriate in a different way. Maybe today it might represent a concrete foundation, on which subsequent musical skyscrapers have been built. After all, the genre directly influenced major artists like Frank Zappa, The Who, and even The Beatles. It produced precursors to ambient music and the mashup genre. And its pioneering techniques – including pitch transposition, looping, and superimposing sounds – have become part of the standard vocabulary of the recording studio.

Like all foundational building blocks, the influence of musique concrète often remains unseen and unacknowledged beneath the surface. But it is still there – holding up everything that has come after. And for those curious to see what supports the musical world around them, all that's needed is a little excavation to descend into that concrete underworld...

1 Halim El-Dabh and the first of the concrete pioneers

Halim El-Dabh was born to the sound of thunder, his arrival heralded by an elemental symphony of snow, hail and lightning that was unprecedented for springtime in Cairo.[1] It seemed almost like nature's cymbal crash, marking the end of an exhaustive family lineage; after all, he was the last of nine children.[2]

A week later, the infant El-Dabh was exposed to another barrage of sound at his naming ceremony. 'All the people sang,' he recalled with improbable clarity years later, at the age of 92. '[S]even times they walked around me when I was only seven days old. That was my earliest exposure to real music.'[3]

Thus, in his first days of life, Halim El-Dabh was confronted with an unusually strong bombardment of sound – both the noises of the environment and the strains of music. Perhaps his addled infant's mind was already forming an experimental

[1] Laurel Myers Hurst, 'Interview with Halim El-Dabh', 1 December 2013, https://astronautapinguim.blogspot.com/2013/12/interview-with-halim-el-dabh.html.

[2] Denise A. Seachrist, *The Musical World of Halim El-Dabh* (Kent: Kent State University Press, 2003), 1.

[3] Hurst.

temperament that would bring them together – inaugurating a new genre, using everyday sounds as its compositional units.

But his penchant for doing things differently may have also had its roots in his peculiar upbringing. Born in 1921 into a wealthy family, El-Dabh grew up in a house full of servants. There was a doorman, two cooks, and several maids. He was even taken to school by a driver in a horse-drawn carriage. Many of the servants lived with the family, bringing into the home their musical instruments and traditional songs from all corners of Egypt.[4]

'My life was really full of music,' El-Dabh would recall years later.[5] The family home was filled with lutes, violins and drums,[6] as well as 'an old, upright monstrosity of a piano' which seemed to fascinate the young boy most. Although his elder siblings had priority over the instrument, El-Dabh would eventually be enrolled in a local conservatory where he learned music theory as well as Beethoven's 'Für Elise' – the obligatory rite of passage for any young pianist.[7]

However, the most influential musical event of his early life also proved transformational for much of Cairo's cultural society. In 1932, King Fu'ad convened a major musical symposium known as the Cairo Congress of Arab Music. This unprecedented event gathered scholars, composers and performers from all over the globe to document, discuss and celebrate music from the Arab world. Brought along by an older brother, El-Dabh caught his first glimpse of a wire recorder

[4]Seachrist, 4–6.
[5]Hurst.
[6]Hurst.
[7]Seachrist, 9.

– the device that would later enable him to create what is now considered the first-ever piece of musique concrète. But it was not just seeing this strange technology that influenced El-Dabh. It was also the way in which it was being used.

El-Dabh was exposed to the wire recorder during a presentation by European composers Béla Bartók and Paul Hindemith. The pair brought the device along to share the field recordings of indigenous music they had gathered on their travels. This must have resonated in the young El-Dabh's mind: more than a decade later, he took this exact approach to gather the raw sound material he needed for his pioneering musique concrète composition.[8]

But for the time being, El-Dabh had other things to focus on. Though music was his great passion, family circumstances were pushing him down a very different career path. El-Dabh's father had made his fortune in the agriculture business, and it seemed destined that his youngest son should follow him. However, for El-Dabh, it was not a classic case of a son being forced into a family profession in which he had no interest. To the contrary – the boy showed enormous enthusiasm for the subject in his own eccentric way. In fact, some of his earliest sound experiments began to take shape in the field of agriculture rather than music.[9]

In particular, El-Dabh became obsessed with an odd idea that sound might be used as an insect repellent to protect crops. As a teenager, he built strange 'sound sculptures' to test

---

[8]Tommy McCutchon, 'Unlimited Americana: A Conversation With Halim El-Dabh', *Music & Literature*, 1 June 2017, https://www.musicandliterature.org/features/2017/6/1/unlimited-americana-a-conversation-with-halim-el-dabh.
[9]Seachrist, 10.

his theory. 'I would take pieces of scrap metal, hang them from a pole, and they would have, like, wings to them,' he recalled. 'When the wind came they would vibrate and hit the pole and create noise.'[10] In later interviews, El-Dabh rarely gave any clues as to whether this peculiar method of pest control actually worked. But the fact that he brought it up so often suggests that it was a formative experience that was perhaps more important for his later musical career than it was for his burgeoning agricultural one.

Strangely, the world of agronomy also exposed El-Dabh to more music and more opportunities for sound experimentation than the local Cairo conservatory. As part of his agricultural studies, El-Dabh travelled to various tiny villages across Egypt. It was his job to advise these communities on optimizing their land use for better crop yields. But wherever he travelled, El-Dabh found himself exposed to music.[11] 'Every time I went somewhere in the country, the people invited the local musicians to meet me,' El-Dabh recalled. There was invariably much singing and dancing, accompanied by a wide array of local instruments. 'I had a wonderful time doing my work and learning music at the same time,' he said.[12]

The agriculture profession also enabled El-Dabh to take his sound experiments with insects to the next level. 'My first exposure to electronic sound devices was back in 1943,' El-Dabh recalled. 'As an agriculturist studying pest control, I wanted to see if sound-emitting devices could control tiny

[10] McCutchon.
[11] Seachrist, 11.
[12] McCutchon.

beetles that attack wheat, corn, alfalfa and beans.' These sound experiments led him to Middle East Radio, a small independent station in Cairo where he obtained a magnetic wire recorder.[13]

With this device in hand, El-Dabh was able to bring together his disparate worlds of interest. The wire recorder enabled him to capture and preserve the folkloric music that was becoming such a formative inspiration for his own ambitions as a composer. But it also allowed him to advance his sound experiments, offering new and untested opportunities for electronic audio manipulation.

El-Dabh decided that one element of traditional music he needed to capture was the *zār*, a secretive all-female healing ceremony. Seemingly oblivious to any social boundaries, El-Dabh disguised himself as a woman in full niqab to infiltrate the group and complete his sonic mission. With the weighty wire recorder hidden under his clothes, he managed to capture the much-desired audio of ceremonial chanting and drumming.[14]

Despite the eccentricity of El-Dabh's cross-dressing escapade, it is what he did next that is most extraordinary. While recordists of the time typically sought to capture and preserve sounds as authentically as possible, El-Dabh wanted to manipulate his audio and find its internal essence. 'I wanted to find the inner sound,' he later explained. 'That's what the

[13] Hurst.

[14] Maha El Nabawi, 'On the Vanguard: The Life and Work of Halim El Dabh', *The National News*, 19 September 2017, https://www.thenationalnews.com/arts-culture/music/on-the-vanguard-the-life-and-work-of-halim-el-dabh-1.629876.

whole idea of electronic music is. You have a recording and you go inside the recording to find the hidden meaning.'[15]

El-Dabh brought his wire recording back to the radio station and used electronic manipulations to play with his sound material. 'I eliminated the fundamental tones of the harmony by changing the voltage,' he said. '[I]t changes the quality of the music, it seeks another quality in the voice, the hidden material, the inner part of the voice.'[16]

He also transformed his recorded sound using acoustic means. 'I even changed the physical qualities of the recording studios by moving panel walls [. . .] altering the subtleties of echo and reverberation to suit me,' El-Dabh explained. 'Then I recorded the resulting sounds on the wire recorder.'[17]

Through his experiments, El-Dabh aimed to erase the identifiable words being sung by the women, as well as the regular beat of the drums, leaving only an abstract impression of the *zār* ceremony. '[I]n the finished recording, the voices are not really recognizable anymore,' El-Dabh summarized. '[O]nly the high overtones, with their beats and clashes, may be heard.'[18]

The result was a ghostly soundscape lasting between 20 and 25 minutes. El-Dabh transferred his composition to magnetic tape and, with that, the first-ever piece of musique concrète was brought into existence.[19]

---

[15]El Nabawi.

[16]El Nabawi.

[17]Hurst.

[18]Thom Holmes, *Electronic and Experimental Music: Technology, Music, and Culture*, sixth edition (New York: Routledge, 2020), 195.

[19]Holmes, 195.

Of course, El-Dabh did not know he was creating a piece of musique concrète at the time – the term did not even exist yet. But his work embodied all the hallmarks of the genre. He had created his composition using recorded sound as his raw material and the studio as his instrument. He had manipulated his recorded sound into something unfamiliar and unrecognizable from its original source. And, he had broken free from the rules of traditional music, such as melody, harmony, rhythm, and meter.

El-Dabh's story seems a classic case of the 'outsider artist'. Working in isolation from the mainstream, without any formal training in studio recording, El-Dabh independently discovered a new way of composing with sound. 'I was carving sound,' he later clarified. 'I used noise like I would a piece of stone.'[20]

In 1944, El-Dabh premiered his pioneering musique concrète composition (which he titled 'The Expression of Zaar') as a sound installation at a local YMCA. 'They had a chamber for me,' El-Dabh recalled. 'People walked in and listened to my music as part of the exhibit'.[21] But for all its innovations, 'The Expression of Zaar' didn't bring El-Dabh much attention. Indeed, that work quickly faded from the public consciousness and languished in obscurity for decades. Rather, it was a piano piece he composed titled 'It Is Dark and Damp on the Front' that launched El-Dabh's music career. When he premiered that piece in 1949, the positive reaction set off a chain of events that would lead El-Dabh to receive a Fulbright scholarship and

---

[20] Margalit Fox, 'Halim El-Dabh, Composer of Martha Graham Ballets, Dies at 96', *New York Times*, 8 September 2017, https://www.nytimes.com/2017/09/08/arts/music/halim-el-dabh-dies.html.

[21] Hurst.

move to the United States the following year.[22] There he would pursue a successful career as a composer, creating the score for Martha Graham's famous ballet 'Clytemnestra' while also working as a professor of music studies at several universities. Today, we are aware of 'The Expression of Zaar' only because of these later successes.

In 2000, a compilation CD of El-Dabh's works was released, *Crossing Into the Electric Magnetic*. While many of El-Dabh's early sound experiments appear to have been lost, a 2-minute excerpt from 'The Expression of Zaar' made its way onto the disc under the title 'Wire Recorder Piece'. Thanks to this excerpt, El-Dabh gradually gained recognition as the composer of the first-ever piece of musique concrète.

The fact that El-Dabh's 'Wire Recorder Piece' could easily have remained in obscurity leads one to question how certain we can be that he was the first musique concrète composer. It seems equally possible that some other outsider artist was experimenting with sound in similar ways, only to have their works lost to time. Indeed, we know of several examples predating El-Dabh's work that could also be considered musique concrète. Some of the most notable come from the world of cinema, which had begun incorporating synchronized sound for feature films from around the mid-1920s. This cinematic audio largely focused on conventional music and diegetic sound effects. But in 1931, director Rouben Mamoulian wanted to try something different for his film *Dr. Jekyll and Mr. Hyde*.

[22] Seachrist, 17 & 20.

The film is best remembered for its transformation scene, in which actor Fredric March devolves from the handsome Dr Jekyll to the simian Mr Hyde in a single take. This visual effect was groundbreaking for the time. But Mamoulian wanted an equally innovative aural effect to complement the onscreen visuals. 'I thought the only way to match the event and create this incredible reality would be to concoct a mélange of sounds that do not exist in nature, that a human ear cannot hear,' Mamoulian explained years later.[23] It's a description that perfectly captures the essence of musique concrète – transforming recorded sounds into something new and unrecognizable.

Many of Mamoulian's techniques in achieving his desired effect also parallel concrete methods. 'Let's record the beat of a gong, cut off the impact, run it backwards,' Mamoulian suggested to his crew, prefiguring the editing and backmasking techniques that would become common among concrete composers.[24]

Where Mamoulian might differ from the concrete aesthetic is in his insistence on rhythm. 'We need some kind of beat,' he maintained. But his solution anticipated another hallmark of musique concrète. 'I ran up and down the stairway,' he explained. 'I put a microphone to my heart and said, "Record it." And that's what is used as the basic rhythm in the scene – the thumping noise which is like no drum on earth because it's the heartbeat, my own heartbeat.'[25]

---

[23] Neil Lerner, 'The Strange Case of Rouben Mamoulian's Sound Stew: The Uncanny Soundtrack in Dr. Jekyll and Mr. Hyde (1931)', in *Music in the Horror Film: Listening to Fear*, ed. Neil Lerner (New York: Routledge, 2010), 70.
[24] Lerner, 70.
[25] Lerner, 70.

Using the sounds of the human body as a material for composition would become a central technique of musique concrète – though these were usually manipulated or decontextualized beyond recognition. Even so, Mamoulian's use of this bodily noise was highly innovative for the time – so much so that it formed a central part of the publicity for the film. 'The beat of the human heart was recorded in Hollywood for talking pictures for the first time,' the Paramount press packet declared.[26]

Like El-Dabh's composition, Mamoulian's work was not recognized as 'pre-musique concrète' until many years later. At the time, his film crew had another name for it. They called it 'Mamoulian's sound stew.'[27]

Beyond Hollywood, another work of 'pre-musique concrète' would be composed a few years later by John Cage, a leading figure in twentieth-century avant-garde music. The score for his 1939 composition *Imaginary Landscape No.1* calls for a muted piano and a large Chinese cymbal. But it also instructs performers to play two test-tone records on the turntables, manipulating the playback speed to achieve different frequencies.[28] When musique concrète was formalized as a genre a decade later, its earliest compositional tool was the turntable. Thus, Cage prefigures this concrete technique by almost 10 years. And the sounds he achieves are also reminiscent of later concrete compositions – from the

[26] Lerner, 68.

[27] Lerner, 70.

[28] John Cage, *Imaginary Landscape No. 1*, https://data-johncage.org//pp/John-Cage-Work-Detail.cfm?work_ID=100.

strange wavering tones of the phonograph machines to the unrecognizable piano sounds.

As these examples illustrate, many maverick artists were already experimenting with sound manipulation and composition long before the genre of musique concrète was officially formalized in the late 1940s. And there may be others, who came even earlier, whose compositions have been lost to time.

In any case, even if the true originator of musique concrète is never definitively identified, the experiments of El-Dabh, Mamoulian and Cage nonetheless illustrate that maverick individuals and outsider artists were the earliest pioneers of the genre. This truth runs counter to the perceived narrative of musique concrète, which places the genre's conception and birth firmly within the organized settings of institutional sound studios. These formal locations would play a key role in developing the genre. But eccentric outsider artists like Halim El-Dabh, who tinkered away in isolation from the musical mainstream, got there first.

A concrete pairing: Halim El-Dabh and The Tornados

You'll never hear Halim El-Dabh's 'Wire Recorder Piece' on the radio. The DJ won't spin it next time you're in the club. And it's probably not on your gym playlist. The same applies to all musique concrète. As an experimental genre pushing the very boundaries of what constitutes music, it is rarely heard by modern audiences. And when it is, the listener often reacts with befuddlement at what appears to be simply a chaotic barrage of noise.

To understand musique concrète today, it helps to place it in the technological context of its time and to pair it with better-known pieces of popular music that share some common feature or even a direct influence.

In the case of 'Wire Recorder Piece', it is important to remember that it premiered in 1944, just 10 years after the first national radio broadcast in Egypt.[29] Before then, for most people in the country, music was largely accessible only in live form, with acoustic instruments. So, for visitors to El-Dabh's sound installation, the eerie and echoey manipulated noises would likely have been received as something entirely new.

Despite this, the work was never going to attract a large audience – due to both its abstract nature and its limited release. But when experimentation and concrete techniques are applied in a more commercial context, they can create new sounds to define a cultural moment, as demonstrated by 'Telstar', the 1962 hit single by The Tornados.

This track was the brainchild of producer Joe Meek. Inspired by television footage transmitted from the Telstar satellite, Meek wrote the instrumental with the aim of developing a new sound to capture the essence of the burgeoning space age.[30]

---

[29] Mustafa Marie, 'Here is Cairo', the 1st Words Ever Spoken Through the Egyptian Radio', *Egypt Today*, 31 May 2022, https://www.egypttoday.com/Article/4/116343/Here-is-Cairo-the-1st-words-ever-spoken-through-the.

[30] Jonathan Sale, 'How Joe Meek's Telstar helped British Pop win the Space Race', *The Times*, 18 December 2012, https://www.thetimes.co.uk/article/how-joe-meeks-telstar-helped-british-pop-win-the-space-race-69tllxldjcx.

A key element of this sound was the clavioline, a kind of early keyboard synthesiser. But Meek also devised his own strange sound effects to pepper throughout his satellite-inspired track. For instance, the song's 'swooshing noises' are believed to be 'a speeded-up recording of a Tube train or a slowed-down recording of tin cans kicked along the floor'.[31] Such techniques display a concrete sensibility: manipulating a recorded sound into something new and unrecognizable.

Meek's mysterious, otherworldly sounds helped propel 'Telstar' to the top of the UK charts in October 1962, displacing Elvis Presley.[32] Two months later, the song topped the American Billboard Hot 100 – making The Tornados the first British band to achieve a US number one.[33] That same week, it was also No. 1 in South Africa and Belgium, and in the top 10 in France, Ireland, Germany, Holland and Sweden.[34] With six million copies sold, 'Telstar' was truly a global sensation.[35]

Despite the enormous gulf in commercial appeal between 'Wire Record Piece' and 'Telstar', both were the products of outsider artists using the recording studio as their primary instrument. Meek was such an outsider that his recording studio was a DIY construction in his London flat. He often had musicians record parts in his bathroom,[36] which served as an

---

[31] Sale.

[32] UK Official Charts, 4 October 1962 – 10 October 1962, https://www.officialcharts.com/charts/singles-chart/19621004/7501/.

[33] Sale.

[34] *Billboard Music Week*, 22 December 1962, 28.

[35] Sale.

[36] Alexis Petridis, 'If Anything Went Wrong, He'd Explode', *The Guardian*, 7 February 2007, https://www.theguardian.com/film/2007/feb/07/popandrock.musicdocumentary.

echo chamber – paralleling El-Dabh's technique of 'moving panel walls within the studio' to adjust the reverberation effect.[37]

Meek's manipulation of his recording equipment was equally unconventional, and again mirrors El-Dabh's experimental approach. Clem Cattini, drummer for The Tornados, recalled one of Meek's innovations: '[H]e put Sellotape around the spindle of the tape recorder so it went slower. When you replayed it, the sound was speeded up.'[38]

But in some respects, Meek's outsider status went even further than El-Dabh's musical eccentricities. As Cattini put it: 'Joe was a musical moron, and I don't mean that disrespectfully. Musically, he didn't know anything.' Indeed, Meek could not play any instruments and was reportedly tone deaf. But, as Cattini concluded, '[H]e was a genius in getting sounds out of that studio.'[39]

Unfortunately, there was also a darker side to Meek's outsider status. 'He was a Jekyll and Hyde character,' David Peters, spokesman for the Joe Meek Appreciation Society, said. 'If anything went wrong, he would explode.' Meek eventually did explode one day in 1967 – murdering his landlady, Violet Shenton, with a shotgun, before turning the weapon on himself.[40]

---

[37] Hurst.

[38] David Gritten, 'Joe Meek and the Tragic Demise of the Maverick Who Revolutionised British Pop', *The Telegraph*, 1 October 2016, https://www.telegraph.co.uk/music/artists/joe-meek-and-the-tragic-demise-of-the-maverick-who-revolutionise/.

[39] Gritten.

[40] Petridis, 'If Anything Went Wrong, He'd Explode'.

Thus, Meek was perhaps the first to establish that sad archetype of the 'mad genius' record producer. But his innovative experiments with 'Telstar' also provide us with a more commercially successful parallel to musique concrète compositions like El-Dabh's 'Wire Recorder Piece'. Both works are products of outsider artists using studio equipment to find new ways to open up recorded sounds. And both would have struck audiences of the time as novel, enabling them to hear a new world of sound for the first time.

But while musique concrète aimed to define an entirely new kind of music – devoid of such hallmarks as rhythm and melody – innovators like Meek combined concrete techniques with the pop music template, creating something both fresh and familiar. And it is in this way that musique concrète survives today. So even if 'Wire Recorder Piece' isn't on your gym playlist, there is likely some more popular track, owing part of its sound to concrete techniques, which is.

For your recommended listening experience, please pair:

'Wire Recorder Piece' by Halim El-Dabh, 1944 (1:58)
with
'Telstar' by The Tornados, 1962 (3:15)

2 Pierre Schaeffer and the age of the manifesto

For the budding aesthete, that early half of the twentieth century was truly the best of times. All over the world, a modernist spirit was inspiring artistic society, with new modes of creative expression being born every day. There was Pablo Picasso and his Cubist paintings, which reassembled the human form; Ezra Pound and his allusion-laden poetry, which influenced everyone from T. S. Eliot to Ernest Hemingway; and Salvador Dalí, whose surreal art reimagined a lobster as a telephone and Mae West's lips as a sofa.

But despite the rich fruits of this creative era, it was also the worst of times. Because alongside each bold, new artistic movement, there inevitably came a ponderous manifesto, defining strict rules for its followers. To accompany Picasso's masterpieces, there were dense treatises from the Cubist clan, pontificating on the tyranny of Euclidean geometry. Alongside his *Cantos*, Pound issued a proscriptive list of 'don'ts' for Imagist poets. And, for every work by Dalí, there seemed to be another iteration of the Surrealist Manifesto.

Today, these tedious texts are condemned to the dusty chambers of chin-stroking academia, while the works associated with their movements live on in wider society. But, in some rare cases, the art has disappeared while the manifesto has lived on.

One example is 'The Art of Noises', a 1913 manifesto which sought to redefine music. Its author was Luigi Russolo, a painter with the Italian Futurist movement. He observed that aside from 'storms, avalanches, and waterfalls, nature is silent'. Evolving in this quietude, the human ear would experience even the simplest sounds of 'a pierced reed or a taut string' as 'something new and wonderful'.[1]

But, with the emergence of the motor car, the factory, and other clamorous products of the machine age, Russolo argued that the modern ear was adapting to very different circumstances. In 'the noisy atmosphere of the great cities', the 'pure sound' of a blown reed or plucked string was losing its power. As evidence, Russolo pointed to the orchestra, which now employed 'three times as many performers' as it had in the eighteenth century, signalling a growing preference for loudness and disharmony.[2]

Russolo concluded that a 'great renewal of music' was needed. He defined six 'families of noises' – from roars and thunderings to whispers and murmurs – which he believed should be integrated into a new music for the industrial age.[3]

Overnight, he abandoned his paintbrush and set to work building mechanical devices to generate noises for his 'futurist orchestra'. These included 'the exploder', which mimicked 'the

[1] Luigi Russolo, 'The Art of Noises', in *The Art of Noises*, trans. Barclay Brown (New York: Pendragon Press, 1986), 23.
[2] Russolo, 'The Art of Noises', 24.
[3] Russolo, 'The Art of Noises', 28.

sound of an internal combustion engine';[4] 'the howler', whose tone hovered 'between that of a traditional string instrument and that of a siren';[5] and 'the crackler', which sounded 'like a cross between a mandolin and a machine gun'.[6]

Russolo gave the first concert of his noise instruments in Milan in 1914. The performance generated such controversy that 'projectiles began to rain upon a still closed curtain' before a single note (or noise) had been played.[7] Once the concert began, the violence escalated, with fights breaking out between Russolo's detractors and supporters. Eventually, half the performers abandoned the stage 'to assault and beat the hostile and hissing audience'.[8]

Despite this mixed reception, Russolo continued to build more noise instruments and planned a tour of Europe. But his plans were scuppered by the First World War.[9] After that conflict, Russolo found some brief demand for his noise machines to accompany silent films, before the advent of sound pictures rendered them obsolete.[10]

When Russolo finally abandoned his musical career, the noise instruments slowly disappeared. Some are believed to have been destroyed in the Second World War. Others simply

[4] James Nice, *A Young Person's Guide to the Avant-Garde* [CD liner notes], LTM Recordings, 2013.
[5] Barclay Brown, 'Introduction', in *The Art of Noises* (New York: Pendragon Press, 1986), 12.
[6] Brown, 4.
[7] Luigi Russolo, 'Polemics, Battles, and the First Performances of the Noise Instruments', in *The Art of Noises*, trans. Barclay Brown (New York: Pendragon Press, 1986), 33.
[8] Russolo, 'Polemics', 34.
[9] Russolo, 'Polemics', 36.
[10] Brown, 9.

vanished.[11] Thus, Russolo's strange music became lost to time, with only two brief samples known to exist, captured on primitive recordings from 1921.[12]

Although Russolo's music died out, the ideas of his manifesto lived on. His writings anticipated the invention of the synthesiser and influenced artists as diverse as proto-concrete pioneer John Cage[13] and British synthpop group Art of Noise, which took its name from his famous text.[14] When Russolo died in 1947, his ideas also appeared to be transmuted into another individual: a French radio engineer named Pierre Schaeffer.

'I have a "Symphony of noises" in mind,' Schaeffer wrote in his journal the following year. But rather than having to build his own noise instruments, like Russolo had, Schaeffer could draw on the resources of a fully equipped radio station. In the sound effects department, he found 'clappers, coconut shells, klaxons' and much more. 'I imagine a scale of bicycle horns,' he enthused.[15]

More significant than these noisemakers, however, was the recording equipment he had access to – microphones, turntables and disc-cutting lathes. This technology was completely inaccessible in Russolo's time, and was equally hard

---

[11] Brown, 10.

[12] Brown, 6.

[13] John Cage, 'List No. 2', in *John Cage: An Anthology*, ed. Richard Kostelanetz (New York: Praeger, 1970), 138.

[14] Imogen Tilden, 'How We Made Art of Noise's Close (to the Edit)', *The Guardian*, 3 July 2018, https://www.theguardian.com/music/2018/jul/03/how-we-made-art-of-noise-close-to-the-edit-anne-dudley-paul-morley.

[15] Pierre Schaeffer, *In Search of a Concrete Music*, trans. Christine North & John Dack (Berkeley: University of California Press, 2012), 4.

to come by for Schaeffer's contemporaries outside of radio studios. Soon, Schaeffer realized that the greatest potential for his 'Symphony of noises' lay with these technologies, rather than his bicycle horns. Because these machines contained new possibilities for carving and manipulating the 'unworked stone'[16] of recorded sound.

Schaeffer's breakthrough came when he used these technologies to cut off the initial sound of a bell being struck. He believed this gave the recording a new quality. As he described it: 'Without its percussion the bell becomes an oboe sound.' Schaeffer later claimed the 'whole of concrete music was contained in embryo in this inherently creative act'.[17]

With this discovery, Schaeffer conceived of an instrument he called 'the most-general-possible piano'. By recording a series of notes on individual discs, and arranging them on their own turntables, he could play melodies by stopping and starting the machines. It was a kind of crude synthesiser. But Schaeffer soon realized the impracticalities of his idea. With only one note per turntable, his invention was 'unwieldy, unsuited to any virtuosity'. Understanding that he would need to surround himself with 'twelve dozen turntables' to fulfil his vision, Schaeffer abandoned the concept.[18]

But in discarding 'the most-general-possible piano', Schaeffer also transcended the restrictions of the twelve-note scale. From this point on, he would conceive a new kind of music unfettered by any conventional attachment to

[16]Schaeffer, 19.
[17]Schaeffer, 7–8.
[18]Schaeffer, 7–10.

melody and meter. Perhaps Schaeffer was able to make this leap because, like Russolo, he was a non-musician. Though his father was a violinist and his mother a singer,[19] Schaeffer was drawn to the literary arts. He considered himself an *écrivain* (a writer), and at 27 had published his first novel.[20] It was his need for a more stable profession that had led him to a degree in radio broadcasting and his work as an engineer.

By the time of his early sound experiments in 1948, Schaeffer had achieved a level of seniority, leading the experimental *Studio d'Essai* (Test Studio).[21] This position enabled him to devote extensive time and resources to his sound research. So, when his next idea for 'a concert of railway engines' struck, it was no problem for a mobile sound unit to accompany him to Batignolles station.

At the trainyard, Schaeffer ordered the drivers 'to improvise' with their engines, while he eagerly recorded 'these mild-mannered whales'. In his journal, he described the apparent distain of the railway workers: 'At their conductors' desks the Batignolles drivers watch me but quickly grow tired,' Schaeffer wrote. 'You can sense that engines can't like being performers.' Nonetheless, he was able to capture enough sound material to return to the studio and begin his composition.[22]

At this point, Schaeffer was still working entirely with turntable technology. This meant he could only edit sounds

[19] Schaeffer, 7.
[20] Christine North, 'Translators' Introduction', in *Treatise on Musical Objects: An Essay Across Disciples* (Berkeley: University of California Press, 2017), xxvi.
[21] Évelyne Gayou, *A Revolution in Music: The History of the Groupe de Recherches Musicales*, trans. David Vaughn (Berkeley: University of California Press, 2025), 15.
[22] Schaeffer, 11.

by playing them back and re-recording them onto a new disc. The process was tedious, 'akin to working only with a film camera to edit a sequence of images'.[23] But despite these challenges, Schaeffer developed several techniques to order and manipulate his sounds.

He created locked grooves – enclosed circles which forced the needle to play a sound fragment on an endless loop. He experimented with volume transitions to allow smoother fades between different noises.[24] He even played sounds backwards – a process which would have probably required rotating the turntable in reverse by hand.[25]

Given its experimental nature, Schaeffer decided that 'symphony' was no longer the appropriate term for his composition. It was a 'study', or rather a series of studies, as his experiments expanded beyond the railway noises to encompass spinning tops, coughing sounds and the clatter of a saucepan lid.[26]

As his studies progressed, Schaeffer began to see the 'inexhaustible potential' contained in every sound. 'I only need to record an empty tin can rolling,' he wrote in his journal. 'I can work from this recording for hours, and the sound is so transposed and unrecognizable that the tin can disappears'.[27]

By the end of his fifth study, Schaeffer believed he had mastered the emergent process of concrete composition.

---

[23]Thom Holmes, *Electronic and Experimental Music: Technology, Music, and Culture*, sixth edition (New York: Routledge, 2020), 218.

[24]Holmes, *Electronic and Experimental Music*, 218.

[25]Holmes, *Electronic and Experimental Music*, 121.

[26]Schaeffer, 15.

[27]Schaeffer, 15.

This final piece combined manipulated fragments of Balinese music with the noises of canal boats and the spinning of tin cans. Schaeffer imagined that listeners would be 'astonished by a composition so skilled, so harmonious, so masterly'.[28]

Using his position at the radio station, Schaeffer got his *Cinq études de bruits* (Five Studies of Noises) on the air in October 1948. As documented in his journal, this broadcast went out 'not on an experimental station, but on the station that was theoretically most popular'.[29]

For all his confidence in the 'masterly' fifth study, Schaeffer nonetheless 'expected complaints'. Instead, he received twelve letters – all of them 'friendly and enlightened'.[30] This response must have been surprising, because Schaeffer's bizarre *études* were unlike anything listeners would have heard before. Moments of musicality arise across their 16 minutes, such as the rhythms of the locked groove loops and a pseudo-melody in the second *étude*. But, for the most part, they are abstract compositions, without the form or structure implicit in traditional music.

Despite the positive reception to his concrete premiere, Schaeffer was forced to abandon his experiments for a year. As part of his senior position at the station, he had to travel on the international conference circuit[31] and to former French colonies to establish new radio outposts.[32] But the foundations

[28] Schaeffer, 20.
[29] Schaeffer, 22.
[30] Schaeffer, 22.
[31] Schaeffer, 21–2.
[32] Christine North & John Dack, 'Translators' Note', in *In Search of a Concrete Music* (Berkeley: University of California Press, 2012), ix.

for his new genre had been set. Schaeffer had even decided on the name for it: musique concrète.

In naming this new kind of music, Schaeffer mirrored the impulse of the age of the manifesto – the desire to define, categorize and restrict an art form. During his year of travel, Schaeffer ruminated further on his emerging theoretical framework for musique concrète. And, on his return, creative ideas were already germinating for his next composition.

Like a true Frenchman, Schaeffer devised the concept for this new piece during a skiing holiday in the Alps.[33] It would be a symphony composed only 'of the noises man can make'. This would include shouting, whistling, breathing, and even the beating of the human heart. He called this project *Symphonie pour un homme seul* (Symphony for a lone man).[34]

Assisting Schaeffer with the composition was Pierre Henry, a young protégé who had joined the studio during Schaeffer's year of intermittent absence. Unlike Schaeffer, Henry was a classically trained musician, having studied under the famous composer Olivier Messiaen at the prestigious Paris Conservatory.[35]

As well as his musicality, Henry also brought the technological adeptness of youth, quickly surpassing Schaeffer's abilities on the turntable. Schaeffer described how Henry 'was making his debut in concrete music with a burst of sound so remarkable that I immediately chose it to round off the *Symphonie* and invalidate its pessimistic title'. This 'invalidation' referred to

[33] Schaeffer, 79.
[34] Schaeffer, 47–9.
[35] James Nice, *The French Avant-Garde in the 20th Century* [CD liner notes], LTM Recordings, 2014.

Henry's introduction of sounds outside the original concept of 'the noises man can make'. One example was Henry's creation of a 'noise like a sawmill' from a manipulated recording of a violin.[36] By the *Symphonie*'s completion, the two Pierres had added many more recordings outside the domain of man – including knocking on doors and prepared piano.[37]

That first collaboration between the pair was fruitful, and *Symphonie pour un homme seul* is now considered the 'first great work of *musique concrète*'.[38] But their next project, a 'concrete opera' based on the Greek myth of Orpheus, proved fraught with difficulty.

At an early performance, Schaeffer recalled that he 'knew better than anyone how bad it was'.[39] When a more complete version premiered in Germany in 1953, the audience response was no more promising – 'I saw Germans laughing', one member of Schaeffer's team recalled.[40] This second collaboration between the two Pierres was simply too ambitious, trying to integrate concrete passages with traditional operatic singing – all without sufficient resources and rehearsal time. Schaeffer would compare the German concert to the French defeat at the Battle of Waterloo.[41] And shortly after, he stepped back from composing.

---

[36] Schaeffer, 58.

[37] Thom Holmes, 'Maximum Turntablism, Part 1', *ThomHolmes.com*, 5 December 2020, https://www.thomholmes.com/post/maximum-turntablism-part-1.

[38] Olivier Julien, *Musique Concrète: 1956–1962* [CD liner notes], Frémeaux & Associés, 2023.

[39] Schaeffer, 99.

[40] Gayou, 171.

[41] Gayou, 172.

Schaeffer returned to his first ambition, as an *écrivain*. He devoted himself to telling the story of musique concrète in a book titled *In Search of a Concrete Music*, signalling his lofty ambitions by referencing one of France's greatest works of literature, Marcel Proust's *In Search of Lost Time*. The early sections of the book showcase Schaeffer's literary prowess by recounting his experimental journey with humour and panache. But the book ends with his 'Outline for a Concrete Music Theory'. Here Schaeffer falls into the technical language of 'harmonic planes' and 'static spatialization', defining a complex vocabulary for musique concrète and rules for how sounds might be classified. This might have been the engineer in Schaeffer coming out; in the book, he even stated that he was 'first and foremost a technician'.[42] But he also grew up at the peak of the age of the manifesto. And so, perhaps it came naturally to him to put a stamp on his artistic movement, to define it irrevocably in ink.

The problem was that Schaeffer's art form was already being passed onto a new generation. And for these young, opinionated artists like Pierre Henry, rules and boundaries would have little meaning.

So perhaps the best of times was already gone for Schaeffer. And now, with the emerging authoritarianism of his manifesto, the worst of times might be ahead . . .

[42] Schaeffer, 95.

A concrete pairing: Pierre Schaeffer and Grandmaster Flash

In the early days of musique concrète, composing with turntables was a crude process. As Pierre Schaeffer remarked, every sound seemed as if it had 'been hacked out with a billhook.'[43] Fortunately, magnetic tape would soon enter the studio, enabling much more precise editing and manipulation.

Even so, phonograph records remained the medium of mass consumption. They could be found in every home. They filled jukeboxes. And they were used to play music live in clubs or over the radio.

This widespread availability of discs, along with gradual improvements in record player technology, enabled a new kind of turntable composition to emerge. It arrived in the late 1970s, as part of the emergence of hip-hop – more than a quarter of a century after Schaeffer's experiments.

One pioneer of this new art was Barbados-born Joseph Saddler, who would assume the name Grandmaster Flash while living in New York.[44] Like Schaeffer before him, Flash was more a technician than a musician. 'I was a scientist,' he reflected years later.[45]

Flash spent his childhood taking electronic appliances apart to see how they worked.[46] As a teenager, he built his

[43] Schaeffer, 18.
[44] Rob Patterson, 'Grandmaster Flash & The Furious Five', *Rock & Roll Hall of Fame 2007* (12 March 2007 programme induction essay).
[45] Andrew Purcell, 'All Hands on Deck', *The Guardian*, 27 February 2009, https://www.theguardian.com/music/2009/feb/27/grandmaster-flash-interview.
[46] Patterson.

own stereo system out of 'parts scavenged from scrapyards and discarded cars'.[47] And he learned how to hotwire public streetlights to power sound systems for outdoor parties.[48]

At events like these, Flash observed the differences among local DJs. Some would transition smoothly between songs – matching the tempo seamlessly – while others moved more clunkily from disc to disc. Enticed by the former approach, Flash began practising turntable techniques at home for hours, hoping to discover more exciting and innovative ways of mixing.[49]

One method he perfected was 'cutting'. This involved cueing up the same song on separate turntables and switching between them at exact moments to extend part of the track – usually a short rhythm break. To support this, Flash even cobbled together his own invention,[50] which he called the 'Peek A Boo System'.[51] With this device, he could privately 'pre-hear' the record on the other deck through headphones, enabling him to cue it in more precisely.

This cutting technique, along with many others, was captured on Flash's seminal recording 'The Adventures of Grandmaster Flash on the Wheels of Steel'. Performed live in the studio, this 7-minute track demonstrated the precise

---

[47] Dorian Lynskey, 'Grandmaster Flash: "Hip-hop's Message was Simple: We Matter"', *The Guardian*, 7 August 2016, https://www.theguardian.com/music/2016/aug/07/the-get-down-baz-luhrmann-grandmaster-flash-hip-hop.

[48] Patterson.

[49] Patterson.

[50] Purcell.

[51] Grandmaster Flash, Twitter (X) post, 18 May 2015, https://x.com/djflash4eva/status/600332233660960769.

timing and versatility of Flash's turntablism, seamlessly mixing songs by Chic, Blondie, Queen and The Incredible Bongo Band.

Though the result is quite different from Schaeffer's work, the basic principles behind many of Flash's techniques mirrored those from the concrete studio. For instance, in *Symphonie pour un homme seul*, Schaeffer and Henry often used repeated sound fragments, in a way that recalls Flash's cutting. One example can be heard at the end of 'Apostrophe', the ninth 'movement' of the *Symphonie*. Here, a female vocal fragment is repeated and layered, extending itself like one of Flash's rhythm breaks.

The major difference between Schaeffer and Flash is how they achieved these effects. Schaeffer's process was entirely studio-bound, requiring patient recording and re-recording of sounds to layer and edit them together. The live element was so absent from Schaeffer's work that he had his audio engineer, Jacques Poullin, build a device to create an illusion of performance. Known as the *potentiometre d'espace*, it consisted of four rings suspended from the ceiling, each connected to a different speaker. By waving his hands before the rings, Schaeffer could shift the sound from speaker to speaker, making him appear like a 'conductor' to his audiences during in-person demonstrations.[52]

Flash's turntablism was the exact opposite. He mixed all his music live and even turned down his initial record deal, believing his performance could never be captured in a studio.[53] Fortunately, Flash eventually relented, and 'The

[52] Holmes, *Electronic and Experimental Music*, 221–2.
[53] Patterson.

Adventures' is now a vital artefact of his legacy as one of the first turntable pioneers.

For Flash, this detail about being first was especially important. 'I don't care who's better, who's worse,' he said. 'My contribution is first. Because first is forever.'[54] And Flash may have been first to master the turntable as an instrument among the 1970s hip-hop generation. But we should also remember that long before he was born, there was a suited French boffin, awkwardly flailing his arms to a very different kind of turntable music.

For your recommended listening experience, please pair:

'Apostrophe' by Pierre Schaeffer & Pierre Henry, 1950 (2:22)
with
'The Adventures of Grandmaster Flash on the Wheels of Steel' by Grandmaster Flash, 1981 (7:07)

[54] Patterson.

3 Pierre Henry and the *Groupe de Recherches de Musique Concrète*

For Pierre Schaeffer, the father of musique concrète, the Second World War didn't end in 1945. '[W]e had driven back the German invasion,' he declared, 'but music was still under an occupying foreign power.'[1]

One of the key enemy headquarters was *Nordwestdeutscher Rundfunk* (Northwest German Broadcasting, or NWDR) in Cologne. This German studio focused on artificially-generated noises. They manufactured bleeps and bloops using oscillators, modulators, and all kinds of electronic gadgetry emerging in the post-war boom. This was the antithesis of Schaeffer's mandate for musique concrète, which advocated for the manipulation of recorded sounds 'ma[de] through listening.'[2]

To fight the growing threat of German domination in electronic music, Schaeffer needed an army. Up to now, his allied unit had consisted of a paltry ragtag team: himself, audio

---

[1]Thom Holmes, *Electronic and Experimental Music: Technology, Music, and Culture*, sixth edition (New York: Routledge, 2020), 234.
[2]David Hirst, 'Schaeffer, GRM and Their Influence on NES-Tools for Max,' in *Proceedings of the Australasian Computer Music Conference 2019* (Melbourne, 2020), 18.

engineer Jacques Poullin, and his young namesake prodigy Pierre Henry.

Finally, in 1951, Schaeffer secured the government funding needed to form 'the first audio studio in the world devoted exclusively to the production of electronic music'.[3] He called it the *Groupe de Recherches de Musique Concrète* (Research Group for Concrete Music, or GRMC). And soon it would attract avant-garde foot soldiers from all over the world.

With the two initialled armies of the NWDR and the GRMC now assembled, the stage was set for another grand international conflict. But, in this era of mutually assured destruction, no shots were fired. Instead, it was a war of words and ideas and overwhelming geopolitical tension. As one composer who worked in both Paris and Cologne, Konrad Boehmer, later reflected: 'You could say that in the Fifties, you had two types of Cold War. One between the Soviet Union and the United States and one between the Cologne studio and the French studio. They disgusted each other.'[4]

Like any good Cold War leader, Schaeffer spent less time among his troops and more on the diplomatic circuit, advocating with foreign powers. He could be away for weeks, delivering lectures and serving as the international ambassador for musique concrète. Schaeffer's absences from the studio were nothing new; he had previously been forced to abandon his musique concrète experiments for about a year following the broadcast of his *Cinq études de bruits* in 1948. But this time,

[3] Holmes, 219.

[4] Jason Gross, 'Interview with Composer Konrad Boehmer', *OHM: The Early Gurus of Electronic Music*, April 2000, https://www.furious.com/perfect/ohm/eimert.html.

the difference was that Schaeffer was 'no longer alone'.[5] As he reflected in his journal, 'On my previous absences, I had put the key under the door cheerfully, without thinking about my return. But the situation had changed.'[6] The studio was now home to a growing militia of experimental composers. And the power vacuum created by Schaeffer's frequent travels might create the opportunity for a coup.

The most likely candidate for such a rebellion was Schaeffer's young namesake protégé: Pierre Henry. Schaeffer's journal entries hint at distrust between them from the very beginning. Schaeffer writes of an 'instinct for power' within Henry, believing that he might be 'predisposed to violence because of his frail appearance'.[7] Those frailties began in childhood. Henry was supposedly so ill that he never attended school.[8] But at age 10, he enrolled in the famous Paris Conservatory, a college for music and dance. He studied under Olivier Messiaen, a composer with a fondness for transcribing birdsong into musical notation. Incorporating the sounds of wildlife into music must have appealed to Henry too. He later stated, 'I think nature was my first influence.'[9]

Henry also credited the sound of 'the train that passed at the rear of the park' as another early inspiration. This aligned

---

[5] Pierre Schaeffer, *In Search of a Concrete Music*, trans. Christine North & John Dack (University of California Press, 2012), 59.

[6] Schaeffer, 59.

[7] Schaeffer, 47.

[8] Will Hodgkinson, 'Soundtrack of My Life: Pierre Henry', *The Guardian*, 15 October 2006, https://www.theguardian.com/music/2006/oct/15/4.

[9] *Pierre Henry: The Art of Sounds* (2006), [Film] Dir. Franck Mallet & Éric Darmon, France: © Mémoire Magnétique / ARTE France / Love Streams agnès b. Productions

him directly with Schaeffer, whose first musique concrète piece was composed of the cries of the engines at the Batignolles station. And, indeed, there 'was a really friendly period' between the pair at the beginning. But the two Pierres were opposed in a more fundamental way. 'For Schaeffer, *musique concrète* was like a musical philosophy which really should not exist as a work,' Henry explained years later. 'As for me, I immediately wanted to create works.'[10]

Henry's productivity in 'creating works' was a source of amazement and concern for Schaeffer. On returning from one trip, he noted that the number of discs in the studio had 'mushroomed dangerously', with his young mentor having 'created extraordinary sound objects by the hundred.'[11] Henry's dominance of the studio was characterized not only by his productivity, but also by the quality of his work. 'Within a few months he had acquired skills in manipulation that amazed even sound engineers,'[12] Schaeffer noted, labelling him a 'turntable genius.'[13]

Henry even began to transform the studio into his own domestic space, with his wife Michèle moving in. As Schaeffer noted, she first visited 'out of curiosity' but soon became 'the mistress of the house.'[14] She took charge of cataloguing the growing collection of discs, using a colour-coded system of 'green, red, blue, and yellow labels.'[15] Although Schaeffer

[10] *Pierre Henry: The Art of Sounds.*
[11] Schaeffer, 69.
[12] Schaeffer, 59.
[13] Schaeffer, 69.
[14] Schaeffer, 59.
[15] Schaeffer, 60.

praised Michèle's 'authority, energy, and kindliness',[16] her cataloguing sowed seeds of disagreement between the father of musique concrète and his young protégé. While Schaeffer believed the sounds should be grouped by source (such as birdsong and train noises), Henry argued for a system based on the character of the sound, using strange titles like *Péripéties* (Incidents) and *Ponctuations* (Punctuations). Henry's approach proved useful for radio broadcasters in search of music and sound effects. So, with this argument seemingly lost, Schaeffer might have begun to feel increasingly like a stranger in his own home.[17]

During Schaeffer's absences, significant technological changes were also taking place. The GRMC acquired its first tape recorders in 1951.[18] But Schaeffer was slow to adapt. His focus on theory and lecturing isolated him from the new methods of composing musique concrète. Meanwhile, Henry's limitless studio time enabled him to charge ahead with this new technology.

During the sessions for Schaeffer and Henry's collaborative concrete opera, *Orphée*, the elder Pierre struggled with the new tape machines. 'The twelve-note tape recorder emits extraneous clunks; the three-track tape recorder is extremely heavy to manipulate; the one with a slider is not set up,' he complained in his journal. 'Only Pierre Henry is comfortable,' he added.[19]

---

[16] Schaeffer, 59.
[17] Holmes, 221.
[18] Holmes, 607.
[19] Schaeffer, 94.

Despite these difficulties, there was no going back. The conveniences of tape would bring a rapid end to the era of turntable composing. Tape machines could play sounds backwards much more smoothly than turntables did. And the somewhat crude 'locked grooves' of Schaeffer's phonograph discs could be replaced by more elegant loops – lengths of tape that were spliced end to end, forming a closed circle that could be repeated endlessly.

Even so, working with tape had its challenges. Edits had to be measured precisely to calculate how many seconds or milliseconds were covered by each centimetre or millimetre of tape. Any cuts required slicing with a razor and splicing the pieces back together using tape or glue. And this had to be done on a special aluminium block to avoid altering the magnetization of the tape.

The transition from disc to tape wasn't the only change taking place at the GRMC. As a first-of-its-kind studio, it was attracting avant-garde composers from all over the world – many with their own ideas and influences, which didn't always align with Schaeffer's restrictive vision.

Curiously, one of the first arrivals came from enemy territory. The young German, Karlheinz Stockhausen, had moved to Paris to study with Henry's ornithologically inclined tutor, Olivier Messiaen.[20] Like Schaeffer (who had been part of the resistance in wartime Paris), Stockhausen had suffered under Nazi rule. His mother was killed as part of the regime's

[20] Holmes, 238.

involuntary euthanasia programme.[21] So now, he was seeking a new kind of music, as different as possible from the Third Reich marching songs he had heard as a boy.[22]

Stockhausen was granted 'a few hours of supervised studio time each week' with the GRMC. But he was so inspired by the possibilities of tape composition, he continued working at his student hostel, despite not being able to hear the results. Stockhausen pounded nails into his desk, using them as spokes to spool his tape reels. He diligently edited his work down to the millimetre.[23] By December 1952, Stockhausen had completed a 3-minute piece, known as his *Konkrete Etüde* (Concrete Study). The eerie composition used recordings of piano strings struck with iron beaters as its source material. 'I copied each sound many times and, with scissors, cut off the attack of each sound,' Stockhausen explained. 'Several of these pieces were spliced together to form a tape loop, which was then transposed to certain pitches using a transposition machine.'[24]

The experience opened up a new world of sounds for Stockhausen, and he was reportedly 'affected for life by the creation of this simple tape piece.'[25] But the young German's work angered Schaeffer. 'He absolutely refused to follow my advice,' Schaeffer recalled. The *Konkrete Etüde* was therefore a disappointment to the father of musique concrète. '[W]e played

---

[21] Michael Kurtz, *Stockhausen: A Biography*, trans. Richard Toop (London: Faber and Faber Limited, 1992), 19.
[22] William L. Weir, *BBC Radiophonic Workshop: A Retrospective* (New York: Bloomsbury Academic, 2023), 105.
[23] Holmes, 238–9.
[24] Holmes, 238.
[25] Holmes, 239.

the tape,' Schaeffer remembered. 'He was terribly pleased with it – me, not at all!'[26]

The result was that Stockhausen returned to Germany, joining the enemy ranks of the NWDR in Cologne.[27] Although fortified by the musical discoveries he had made with the GRMC, the experience left Stockhausen with a bad aftertaste. As Konrad Boehmer recalled: 'When Stockhausen entered the Cologne studio shortly after that, he behaved like somebody who didn't want to talk about Paris.'[28]

Another visitor to the GRMC around the same time stood in stark contrast to Stockhausen. Unlike the young German, Edgard Varèse was coming to the end of his career and sported the wild white hair and bushy eyebrows of a mad old composer. In fact, Varèse was so advanced in years that he had once been an acquaintance of the Italian Futurist Luigi Russolo, whose manifesto 'The Art of Noises' had been written before most musique concrète practitioners were even born.[29]

While Schaeffer drove Stockhausen out for straying too far from his vision, Varèse found a collaborator at the GRMC in Pierre Henry. Together, they would assemble the world's first composition combining magnetic tape and orchestra.[30]

Varèse had been working on this piece, known as *Déserts*, since 1950. He conceived of it in seven parts: four for orchestra

---

[26] Kurtz, 55–6.

[27] Kurtz, 56.

[28] Gross.

[29] Barclay Brown, 'Introduction', in *The Art of Noises* (New York: Pendragon Press, 1986), 9–10.

[30] "Blue" Gene Tyranny, 'Déserts for Brass, Percussion, Piano & Tape', *AllMusic*, https://www.allmusic.com/composition/d%C3%A9serts-for-brass-percussion-piano-tape-mc0002358248.

and three for magnetic tape. The title referred to a vision Varèse had in mind when composing the piece – 'images of the deserts of Earth [. . .] but above all, the deserts in the mind of humankind.'[31]

By 1954, the work was still unfinished. So Varèse moved from his simple home studio in New York to the well-equipped workspaces of the GRMC in Paris.[32] In October and November of that year, Henry assisted Varèse in bringing the tape portions of his composition to completion.[33] Then, in December, *Déserts* had its premiere at the Théâtre des Champs-Élysées. GRMC member Philippe Arthuys performed the tape sections under the technical direction of Henry.[34]

Despite the productivity of Varèse and Henry's collaboration, the audience reaction to this revolutionary work was hostile. As one reviewer reported, '[T]he work was often unaudible [*sic*] through the barrage of stamping, clapping, and catcalls that arose.'[35] Perhaps it was a poor omen that the theatre selected for the performance was the same venue that premiered Igor Stravinsky's *The Rite of Spring*, a ballet which caused the most famous riot in classical music history.

Varèse was so upset by the reaction that it 'reportedly drove him to tears.'[36] But he remained determined. He returned to

---

[31] Tyranny.
[32] Holmes, 200.
[33] Son/Ré association, 'Deserts – Interpolations', *Pierre Henry*, https://pierre-henry.org/items/show/1744.
[34] Évelyne Gayou, *A Revolution in Music: The History of the Groupe de Recherches Musicales*, trans. David Vaughn (Berkeley: University of California Press, 2025), 173.
[35] Holmes, 201.
[36] Holmes, 201.

the GRMC that night to remix the tapes before embarking on further live performances, including one with the young Stockhausen at the volume controls.[37]

This poor reception for Varèse's *Déserts* shouldn't have been a surprise – it reflected a broader existential anxiety about machine-generated music. As one critic wondered in 1955:

> We ask ourselves whether truly this is the beginning of a new world or whether perhaps the world, whether our cultural world, is about to perish. There are people who earnestly and seriously fear this, where music becomes the slave of the machine, or, where, if you will, technical progress takes hold of art.[38]

In this context, the war between the Paris and Cologne schools should have felt futile. After all, both were advocating for a new kind of music, incorporating the infinite sounds of the electronic ecosystem. And they had a common enemy among the cultural critics who were fearful of their work. But rather than cooperating towards a mutual mission, the two studios allowed their minor differences to fuel animosity and distrust.

By this time, the antagonism of small divisions was also bubbling up within the GRMC. Schaeffer's concerns began to shift away from his Cold War with the Germans and more towards preventing a civil war in his own ranks. Again, it was a question of dogma. Soon after the premiere of *Déserts*, Henry

---

[37] Holmes, 201.

[38] Otto Luening, 'Origins', in *The Development and Practice of Electronic Music*, ed. Jon H. Appleton & Ronald C. Perera (Englewood Cliffs: Prentice-Hall Inc., 1975), 15.

had started producing artificial sounds using oscillators, the tool of the rival NWDR studio at Cologne.[39] For Schaeffer, this was anathema.

On top of this, there was supposedly 'some resentment, by Schaeffer, of the success being enjoyed by Pierre Henry'.[40] The young composer had already created 'the first *musique concrète* to appear in a commercial film'.[41] And now he was beginning a fertile collaboration with famed choreographer Maurice Béjart on a series of concrete ballets.

In the end, Henry leaving was the only way to avoid a civil war. One member of the GRMC, Luc Ferrari, was at the fateful meeting in 1958 where the sundering of the two Pierres finally took place. 'Pierre Henry stood up, gave Schaeffer a letter, and then left with his entire team,' Ferrari recalled. '[H]e told Schaeffer: "I disagree with your creative approach, with your pedagogy, I disagree with everything." Then, bang! He was gone.'[42]

But even if the rebellious agent had been excised, Schaeffer could not destroy his ideas. Henry was now a free man. He could take the concrete techniques he had learned at the GRMC and apply them to whatever context or type of music he desired.

If the Cold War analogy can stretch so far, Henry's departure (and other events to come in 1958) might be equivalent to the

[39] Hirst, 18.
[40] Hirst, 16.
[41] James Nice, *The French Avant-Garde in the 20th Century* [CD liner notes], LTM Recordings, 2014.
[42] Jacqueline Caux, *almost nothing with Luc Ferrari*, trans. Jérôme Hansen (Berlin/Los Angeles: Errant Bodies Press, 2012), 27.

fall of the Iron Curtain. It wasn't exactly McDonald's coming to Moscow. But the two ideologies of the Paris and Cologne schools would never be quite so separate again. Now, the Parisien form of musique concrète was free to seep across borders, blending into other modes and genres of music and reaching wider audiences than ever before. And it would never return to the purity of Schaeffer's original vision.

A concrete pairing: Pierre Henry and Imogen Heap

Upon leaving the GRMC in 1958, Pierre Henry did what most jobless youngsters would: he moved back in with his parents. But rather than reoccupying his old bedroom as a living space, he turned it into a private studio. Without missing a beat, Henry continued where he left off at the GRMC, completing two compositions from his bedroom before the year was over.[43]

In 1959, Henry moved out and founded his own studio, known as Studio Apsome.[44] Liberated from the strictures of the GRMC, he experimented more heavily with sounds outside the concrete domain. In fact, the first piece he made at Studio Apsome, *Investigations*, was composed entirely of artificial sounds 'created from a frequency generator'.[45]

---

[43] Son/Ré association, 'Studio Zéro', *Pierre Henry*, https://pierre-henry.org/studios/studio-0.

[44] Son/Ré association, 'Studio Apsome 1', *Pierre Henry*, https://pierre-henry.org/studios/studio-apsome-1.

[45] Son/Ré association, 'Investigations', *Pierre Henry*, https://pierre-henry.org/items/show/174.

But despite his openness to new modes of sonic development, Henry stayed in touch with the roots of his concrete foundations. In 1963, he returned to the raw material of recorded sound and created one of the purest pieces of musique concrète ever made – *Variations pour une porte et un soupir* (Variations for a Door and a Sigh).

This work was pure concrete in the sense that it drew from a minimum number of sources, manipulating them in myriad ways to open up a much broader sound profile. As the title implies, these sources were the squeaking of a door and the gentle sigh of the human breath. Added to this, Henry also included the noises of a musical saw.[46]

For part of his sequence, titled 'Vagues' (Waves), Henry drew entirely on recordings of the human breath. Taking this softest sound imaginable, he layered and amplified it until it recalled the most majestic and powerful forces of nature – roaring winds and crashing waves.

Within popular music, very few songs are constructed from such a minimal sonic palette. On the rare occasions in which they are, there is little hope that they can become hits. When singer-songwriter Imogen Heap tried to promote a track she constructed using only her voice, a radio executive told her, '[T]hat song is never going to connect, people are never going to like it.'[47]

[46] Jacques Longchampt, *Variations pour une porte et un soupir/Voile d'Orphée* [CD liner notes], Harmonia Mundi, 1994.

[47] Samantha Leach, 'Imogen Heap's "Hide And Seek" Is Still The Go-To Song for Teen Dramas, 15 Years Later', *Bustle*, 20 February 2024, https://www.bustle.com/p/imogen-heaps-hide-seek-is-still-the-go-to-song-for-teen-dramas-15-years-later-22915684.

But Heap's song, 'Hide and Seek', was not as sonically one-dimensional as it sounds. Like Henry, she took her single sound source, electronically processed it, and layered the results on top of each other. In this way, she transformed her lone voice into a polyphonic alien choir.

Heap achieved this effect using a vocal harmonizer.[48] This electronic equipment enables lone singers to harmonize with themselves using automatically synthesized voices. But Heap also embellished the track with some further concrete flourishes. 'I actually copy and pasted quite a lot of the breathing into the final version,' she explained, referring to the process as 'building air around' the track.[49]

Despite the reservations of the radio executive, Heap's song became a huge hit on release in 2005. This was driven largely by a featured spot on American teen drama *The O.C.* Since then, the song has 'soundtracked climactic moments in a number of dramas about adolescents'. It was also prominently sampled for Jason Derulo's number one hit 'Whatcha Say', which took its title from a key line in Heap's original.[50]

Heap's subsequent recordings have demonstrated an even clearer concrete sensibility. Most notably, her 2014 album *Sparks* drew on '900 found-sound snippets' crowdsourced from fans. These included everything from 'the manipulated noise from a slinky' to 'her niece's heartbeat' (sent in by her brother).[51]

---

[48] Leach.

[49] Tom Cridland, '#259 - Imogen Heap Interview: making Hide and Seek', [Video interview], 4 May 2021, https://www.youtube.com/watch?v=-Scn74BnDz4&ab_channel=TomCridland.

[50] Leach.

[51] Cat Zhang, 'The Eternal Influence of Imogen Heap', *Pitchfork*, 8 August 2022, https://pitchfork.com/features/article/imogen-heap-eternal-influence/.

But 'Hide and Seek' has a further concrete secret hidden in the mix. Right at the end of the track is a mysterious kind of white noise, which most listeners can only hear by cranking up the volume. 'My studio was next to a train line,' Heap later explained.[52] 'Late at night there was a train and it went past and it harmonized itself.'[53]

Heap's train harks back to Henry's early influence of 'the train that passed at the rear of the park'. It also recalls Pierre Schaeffer's engines at the Batignolles station for his *Cinq études de bruits*. Is it just a coincidence? Or is it a cosmic alignment of the concrete fates? Whatcha say?

For your recommended listening experience, please pair:

'Vagues' by Pierre Henry, 1963 (1:36)
with
'Hide and Seek' by Imogen Heap, 2005 (4:28)

---

[52]Cridland.
[53]Leach.

4 Iannis Xenakis and the 1958 Brussels World's Fair

Today, you only have to press 'play' to have any sound injected directly into your ears – anytime, anyplace. But before this was possible, every moment of music was a live performance. So, it was often composed with specific locations in mind.

In the Palaeolithic era, Stone Age man was making staging areas in caves 'where speech, song, or instrumental performance would be amplified most powerfully or pleasingly'.[1] As civilization developed, music entered the workplace: sailors sang sea shanties while raising the rigging, and farmers chanted *a cappella* tunes in agricultural fields. When the lofted ceilings of the cathedrals were raised across Europe, they offered a home for new kinds of choral music, while the eighteenth-century concert halls made room for the expansion of the orchestra. Even after the invention of recording technologies, music continued to be composed with performance spaces in mind. Just think of the arena rock of bands like Queen, Journey and Bon Jovi.

[1] Mark Katz, *Music and Technology: A Very Short Introduction* (Oxford: Oxford University Press, 2022), 51.

But what location does musique concrète belong to? That strangely ethereal music, with no instruments and no performers, feels particularly homeless. Perhaps it is telling that the earliest composition by Pierre Schaeffer, the father of the genre, debuted over radio – piped into countless locations at once, with no single space to call its own.

But a decade after that first broadcast, an opportunity finally arose to build a home for musique concrète. It came through the Philips Radio Corporation. The company was eager to construct a pavilion for the 1958 Brussels World's Fair, an international exhibition expected to attract millions of visitors from across the globe. They wanted an impressive space that could host a multimedia experience, demonstrating the power of the company's audio equipment. The Philips team initially thought a bit of Benjamin Britten could provide the appropriate soundtrack.[2] But their Swiss-French architect, Charles-Édouard Jeanneret, had a very different kind of music in mind.

Known by the mononym Le Corbusier, the architect was one of the most important practitioners in his field. Today, he is remembered as a pioneer of the modernist style, with seventeen of his buildings inscribed on UNESCO's World Heritage List.[3]

---

[2] Kees Tazelaar, 'An Austrian in Eindhoven: Anton Buczynski and the Recording of *Le poème électronique*', in *Inside Le Corbusier's Philips Pavilion: A Multimedia Space at the 1958 Brussels World's Fair*, ed. Peter Wever (Rotterdam: nai010 publishers, 2015), 83.

[3] UNESCO World Heritage List, 'The Architectural Work of Le Corbusier, an Outstanding Contribution to the Modern Movement', 2016, https://whc.unesco.org/en/list/1321/.

Le Corbusier also happened to be a fan of Edgard Varèse, the wild-haired old composer whose mix of orchestral and tape music had attracted boos at the Théâtre des Champs-Élysées in 1954. (The architect had even been in the audience that night.[4]) But unlike the jeering masses, Le Corbusier was spellbound by these new sounds. Reportedly, he considered Varèse 'the only composer' of the twentieth century.[5] So, he accepted the Philips project on the condition that Varèse's strange music was included.[6]

But there was a slight problem: Le Corbusier had already been contracted to build an entire city in India.[7] So, after sketching a simple floor plan for the Philips Pavilion, he was forced to leave the next stage of the work to Iannis Xenakis, an assistant in his firm who also had a penchant for the avant-garde.

Like Pierre Schaeffer, Karlheinz Stockhausen, and many others in the musique concrète orbit, Xenakis bore the scars of the Second World War. In his native Greece, he had 'engaged in the resistance against the Nazis', spending a few spells in prison.[8] When the Greek Civil War erupted in 1946, Xenakis

[4]Thom Holmes, *Electronic and Experimental Music: Technology, Music, and Culture*, sixth edition (New York: Routledge, 2020), 202.
[5]Norma Beecroft, *Conversations With Post World War II Pioneers of Electronic Music*, promotional copy (Canadian Music Centre, 2015), 23.
[6]Peter Wever, 'The Decorators: The Creation of the Light Effects in *Le poème électronique*', in *Inside Le Corbusier's Philips Pavilion: A Multimedia Space at the 1958 Brussels World's Fair*, ed. Peter Wever (Rotterdam: nai010 publishers, 2015), 49.
[7]Ludo van Halem, 'Introduction', in *Inside Le Corbusier's Philips Pavilion: A Multimedia Space at the 1958 Brussels World's Fair*, ed. Peter Wever (Rotterdam: nai010 publishers, 2015), 9.
[8]Beecroft, 15.

took a shrapnel blast to the face, losing an eye and gaining a scar that would remain with him for life.[9]

Exiled from the country and sentenced to death as a revolutionary, Xenakis ended up in Paris.[10] He was drawn to the French capital because of his love of music. (Later, he described music as 'the only thing that I thought was still pure' after his dreadful wartime experiences.[11]) Xenakis even harboured ambitions of becoming a composer himself. But he also needed money.

At Le Corbusier's office, he found a steady job. While most penniless refugees would be thrilled at the opportunity of stable employment with a world-famous architect, Xenakis was apathetic. 'I didn't care for architecture,' he reflected years later.[12]

Still, Le Corbusier and Xenakis shared an interest in experimental music. And the young Greek was able to indulge this passion outside the workplace. He studied with Olivier Messiaen, who also taught Pierre Henry and Karlheinz Stockhausen.[13] Xenakis even attended the concerts of Pierre Schaeffer and his musique concrète crowd. But he felt there was room for improvement. 'I didn't like very much the sounds

---

[9] Liam Cagney, 'The genius of Iannis Xenakis', *The Spectator*, 5 March 2022, https://www.spectator.co.uk/article/the-genius-of-iannis-xenakis/.

[10] Tom Service, 'A Guide to Iannis Xenakis's Music', *The Guardian*, 23 April 2013, https://www.theguardian.com/music/tomserviceblog/2013/apr/23/contemporary-music-guide-xenakis.

[11] Beecroft, 19.

[12] Beecroft, 20.

[13] Jiri Slabihoudek, 'With a Sound Forged in War, Iannis Xenakis Embraced Chaos', *New York Times*, 24 September 2022, https://www.nytimes.com/2022/09/22/arts/music/iannis-xenakis-centennial.html.

that they produced,' Xenakis said. 'I thought they were too unorganized.'[14]

As part of the Philips project, Xenakis would have the opportunity to make some better 'organized' sounds of his own, composing a musique concrète piece to serve as an interlude. But first, he had to design the house for it.

Alongside his basic floor plan, Le Corbusier had left a few ideas for Xenakis to start from. He had declared that the pavilion should be shaped like a stomach, to mirror the transformative process that visitors would experience as they passed through.[15] On reflection, it was perhaps an unflattering metaphor to describe the effect of Varèse's music on audiences. And another of Le Corbusier's descriptions was equally off-putting. 'It must feel as if they're entering a slaughterhouse,' he said. 'In: bang, a blow to the head, and out.'[16]

Working from this rough vision, Xenakis created the initial drawings for the pavilion in October 1956.[17] Perhaps inspired by the mathematical heritage of his homeland, Xenakis based his design around 'hyperbolic paraboloids'.[18] When he translated this into the first scale model, using string and piano wire on a wooden frame, it resembled a kind of distorted saddle.[19]

---

[14] Beecroft, 23.
[15] van Halem, 12.
[16] van Halem, 13.
[17] Peter Wever, 'Pavilion without a Façade: Le Corbusier Versus Gerrit Rietveld', in *Inside Le Corbusier's Philips Pavilion: A Multimedia Space at the 1958 Brussels World's Fair*, ed. Peter Wever (Rotterdam: nai010 publishers, 2015), 21.
[18] Wever, 'Pavilion without a Façade', 21.
[19] Peter Wever, 'Woman's Hairpins Help to Build Architecture of the Future: An Unlikely Tale of the Conception of the Philips Pavilion', in *Inside Le Corbusier's Philips Pavilion: A Multimedia Space at the 1958 Brussels World's Fair*, ed. Peter Wever (Rotterdam: nai010 publishers, 2015), 34.

In the traditional narrative of the Philips Pavilion, its now legendary architecture is credited entirely to Le Corbusier's genius. One New York newspaper even conjured a myth that Le Corbusier had built the first scale model himself, using his maid's hairpins after being struck by a sudden flash of inspiration as she entered the room.[20] And when Philips issued its press file on the pavilion, Xenakis was completely overlooked.[21]

In reality, the process of developing the pavilion was much more collaborative. And once Xenakis and Le Corbusier's final design was completed together, the construction could begin. Perhaps appropriately for a building that would bring musique concrète to the masses, the structure was made of concrete. Its exterior was supported by bracing wires and the whole thing was covered in a 'high-gloss aluminium paint'.[22] The finished construction stood over twenty metres tall.[23] The Philips press file compared its unusual form to 'a giant shell of bizarre shape from some exotic seabed'.[24]

But, of course, the building was only part of the spectacle. While the pavilion was under construction in Belgium, Varèse

---

[20] Wever, 'Woman's Hairpins Help to Build Architecture of the Future', 35.

[21] Peter Wever, 'Notes', in *Inside Le Corbusier's Philips Pavilion: A Multimedia Space at the 1958 Brussels World's Fair*, ed. Peter Wever (Rotterdam: nai010 publishers, 2015), 160.

[22] Peter Wever, 'Colour in the Philips Pavilion: Le Corbusier's Use of *Types Couleurs*', in *Inside Le Corbusier's Philips Pavilion: A Multimedia Space at the 1958 Brussels World's Fair*, ed. Peter Wever (Rotterdam: nai010 publishers, 2015), 38.

[23] Wever, 'Notes', 152.

[24] Philips, 'The "Electronic Poem" in the Philips Pavilion: A Rich and Rare Experience of a World of Wonder', in *Inside Le Corbusier's Philips Pavilion: A Multimedia Space at the 1958 Brussels World's Fair*, ed. Peter Wever (Rotterdam: nai010 publishers, 2015), 115.

was across the border in the Netherlands, putting together a new composition at the Philips Research Laboratories.[25] This work, called *Poème électronique* (Electronic Poem), would be the soundtrack to the pavilion's multimedia show. Just like his previous work, this piece blended styles that had previously been segregated. In this case, it was the rival doctrines of electronic music from France and Germany – the manipulation of recorded sound favoured by Pierre Schaeffer's musique concrète, as well as the artificial tone generation of the Cologne studio.

But the Philips Board of Directors had their doubts. They didn't understand Varèse's strange music. When they heard an early excerpt of his weird composition, they tried to remove him from the project. Only a curt response from Le Corbusier in India enabled him to stay onboard. 'There cannot for a moment be a question of giving up Varèse,' Le Corbusier wrote. 'If that should happen, I will withdraw from the project entirely.'[26]

Chastened, the Board allowed Varèse to continue. But they might have been justified in harbouring doubts. When he had arrived at the studio in September 1957, Varèse had estimated that his work would be done in a few weeks. But after more than 5 months, only half the piece was completed.[27] And Varèse's eccentricities were causing issues with the studio workers too.

[25] Holmes, 204.
[26] Holmes, 204.
[27] Tazelaar, 85.

Anton Buczynski, a technician who was assisting Varèse, was especially baffled by the unconventional score that had been written to guide the composition process. 'It was a piece of brown paper, wrapping paper, with lines, zigzag figures and waves drawn on it,' he recalled. 'I was mystified. And whenever a new sound had been created, he [Varèse] would rub something out and draw something else in its place.'[28]

Sourcing the recorded sounds for the piece was also challenging. 'Varèse wanted fighter jets,' Buczynski recalled. Unable to produce this sound synthetically, he and his team had to convince the commander of a nearby airbase to arrange a flyby. '[W]e were still hauling the microphones up to the roof and there they came, three of them! Too early.' The commander refused another flyby because of the expense. So Buczynski and his team were forced to leave their equipment on the roof, protected by an umbrella, until another plane passed a few days later.[29]

There were challenges in Paris too, where Xenakis was working on his own composition. This short piece would play during audience changeovers between performances of the *Poème électronique* at the pavilion. Unlike Varèse, whose composition was a fusion of styles, Xenakis was creating a work of pure musique concrète. He had chosen the crackle of burning charcoal as his sound material. According to one collaborator, '[W]e nearly set the studio on fire and died of asphyxiation.'[30]

---

[28]Tazelaar, 85.

[29]Tazelaar, 87.

[30]Pierre Arnaud & Peter Wever, 'Shadowplay: Pierre Arnaud's Replacement Show for the Philips Pavilion', in *Inside Le Corbusier's Philips Pavilion: A Multimedia*

But despite this brush with death, Xenakis judged the finished piece to be 'very good'.[31]

By this time, it was just a few weeks before the opening of the World's Fair. And while most exhibitors were putting the final touches to their displays, Varèse was still working on the *Poème électronique*. When the World's Fair officially opened on 17 April 1958, the pavilion remained closed. Philips representatives arranged an opening ceremony for 22 April, using an incomplete version of the *Poème*, but then immediately shut down again. Further delays were caused when rats chewed through the cables inside the building. Eventually, the Philips Pavilion officially opened to the public on 20 May – more than a month into the 6-month exhibition.[32]

Once opened, the pavilion gave three performances per hour, accommodating up to 500 people at a time.[33] Visitors entered a cavernous chamber through an entry passage that was sealed off before the performance began. The room was plunged into darkness as the arrhythmic bleeps and squawks of Varèse's *Poème électronique* echoed through some 400 loudspeakers.[34] The 8-minute composition was

Space at the 1958 Brussels World's Fair, ed. Peter Wever (Rotterdam: nai010 publishers, 2015), 80–1.

[31] Wever, 'Notes', 157.

[32] Peter Wever, 'Inside the Philips Pavilion: Personal Stories from Those Who Operated *Le poème électronique*', in *Inside Le Corbusier's Philips Pavilion: A Multimedia Space at the 1958 Brussels World's Fair*, ed. Peter Wever (Rotterdam: nai010 publishers, 2015), 91.

[33] Peter Wever, 'Like Ants in a Hurricane: One and a Half Million Visitors to the Philips Pavilion', in *Inside Le Corbusier's Philips Pavilion: A Multimedia Space at the 1958 Brussels World's Fair*, ed. Peter Wever (Rotterdam: nai010 publishers, 2015), 123.

[34] Philips, 118.

accompanied by film images of past cultures, moving up to the present day, with pictures of 'engineers, atom bombs, telescopes and architecture'.[35] There were several other visual elements too, including lighting effects representing 'a red sun, a moon, stars, clouds and lightning'.[36] At the end, the lights were raised and a separate exit was opened, mirroring Le Corbusier's vision of the pavilion as a stomach – with the audience entering through one passage, 'digesting' the performance in a central chamber, and exiting through a second passage.

More than 3,000 performances of the *Poème électronique* were given during the course of the World's Fair.[37] Philips estimated that 1.5 million visitors attended the multimedia show, though this figure seems to assume maximum capacity for every performance.[38] Nonetheless, the pavilion arguably exposed more people to musique concrète than ever before – both in the pure form of Xenakis' interlude music and in the electronic fusion of Varèse's main event. But what did audiences think?

As one of the world's first multimedia experiences for a mass audience, it certainly offered a novel sensory spectacle. Some visitors were reportedly so scared that they wet themselves. At one performance, the sights and sounds induced labour in a heavily pregnant woman.[39] But one visitor captured

[35]Wever, 'The Decorators', 50.
[36]Wever, 'The Decorators', 59.
[37]Wever, 'Like Ants in a Hurricane', 123.
[38]Wever, 'Notes', 160.
[39]Wever, 'Inside the Philips Pavilion', 96.

the general sentiment perfectly: 'It is impressive, but do I understand it? No, not really.'[40]

Some Philips staff felt the same. Despite being present for hundreds (if not thousands) of performances, one projectionist admitted he 'never really understood much of it'. Another technician realized that the film and music 'dealt with a vision of man's development'. But he felt 'the story was presented in a rather infantile way.'[41]

Nonetheless, the spectacle at the Philips Pavilion generated a huge amount of publicity and garnered praise in the media. Even Varèse, who had been wounded by the critical reaction to his previous work, was the recipient of some adulation. In fact, when the *Poème électronique* premiered in the United States later that year, its reception seemed to signal a change of heart in the critical anxieties towards electronic music. '[W]ild as the sounds seem to us now, it is hard to doubt a future for such means of composition,' one critic wrote. 'In a world of jet planes, man-made moons, atomic submarines, and hydrogen bombs, who is to say this music does not have a place?'[42]

Even more important than the critics, however, were the experimental musicians. And a whole new generation of them passed through Le Corbusier's stomach. There was Delia Derbyshire, who would soon join the famous BBC Radiophonic Workshop and develop the theme music for *Doctor Who*. Ralf Hütter attended as well, 12 years before forming the pioneering

[40]Wever, 'Like Ants in a Hurricane', 136.
[41]Wever, 'Inside the Philips Pavilion', 99.
[42]Holmes, 206.

electronic band Kraftwerk.[43] Established avant-gardists were there too. Karlheinz Stockhausen, who had worked at both the Paris and the Cologne studios, visited. So did Luc Ferrari, a recent recruit to Pierre Schaeffer's circles, and John Cage, the American maverick credited with producing 'one of the earliest examples of *[m]usique concrète*'.[44]

With this coming together of experimental composers from around the world, perhaps the Philips Pavilion symbolized a monument to peace. It was not just a home for musique concrète. It was a home for all electronic music. But unfortunately, the contractual agreement stipulated that Philips had to restore the grounds of the pavilion to their original state after the fair was over. And that meant destroying Xenakis and Le Corbusier's creation.[45]

One of the directors at Philips was keen to create a publicity stunt out of the demolition. Understanding that the bracing wires had to be broken first, he proposed exploding a hydrogen-filled balloon inside the pavilion, so that the pressure would cause the wires to snap. Another suggestion was to run an electric current through them, so they 'would become red-hot and the pavilion would cave in like a pudding'.[46]

---

[43] William L. Weir, *BBC Radiophonic Workshop: A Retrospective* (New York: Bloomsbury Academic, 2023), 29.

[44] Klaus George Roy, 'The Strange and Wonderful Sonic World of John Cage', *HiFi/Stereo* Review, November 1960, 64.

[45] Peter Wever & Kees Tazelaar, 'Beyond the Final Performance: Demolition of the Philips Pavilion', in *Inside Le Corbusier's Philips Pavilion: A Multimedia Space at the 1958 Brussels World's Fair*, ed. Peter Wever (Rotterdam: nai010 publishers, 2015), 140.

[46] Wever & Tazelaar, 141.

In the end, it was decided to simply send workers up on ladders to cut the wires one by one. Despite some ominous creaking, the pavilion remained defiantly standing – as if the spirit of musique concrète could not quite abandon its home just yet. But then, in February 1959, the whole thing was blown up with dynamite.[47]

And so, musique concrète was left homeless again. But this displaced state brought with it a kind of freedom. Because when one has nowhere to go, one can go anywhere. And musique concrète was certainly going places . . .

A concrete pairing: Iannis Xenakis and Björk

Despite his significant contribution to the architectural design of the Philips Pavilion, Iannis Xenakis was eclipsed by the more famous Le Corbusier. And the Greek composer's musical input was equally overshadowed by Edgard Varèse. But while the *Poème électronique* was the main event, Xenakis' musique concrète interlude was just as radical in its own way.

Up until that point, the musique concrète of Pierre Schaeffer and his *Groupe de Recherches de Musique Concrète* (GRMC) was characterized by abrupt changes between sounds. But Xenakis found their approach 'unorganized'. As a counter to this prevailing style, his piece for the Philips Pavilion had almost no variation in dynamics or texture across its 3-minute runtime.

[47] Wever & Tazelaar, 144.

Unlike most musique concrète, it was calm and comforting, sounding something like raindrops falling on a tin roof.

The work (later titled 'Concret PH') was created entirely from the sounds of burning charcoal. Xenakis transformed this source material by cutting several one-second fragments out of the recordings. He manipulated each section of tape by varying its speed or using filters to give it a metallic sound. The fragments were then reordered and spliced back together to create the finished piece.[48]

Working with sounds at this microscopic level would become a hallmark of Xenakis' musical philosophy. Years later, he coined the term 'microsound'.[49] More significantly, he was also credited as an originator of 'granular synthesis'.[50] This involves working with minute 'grains' of sounds to unlock all kinds of manipulations that were previously thought impossible, such as speeding up or slowing down a recording without altering its pitch.

At the time of 'Concret PH', this type of work could only be done by painstakingly cutting up small slices of tape and piecing them back together by hand. But once digital technologies became available, composers could start to 'zoom in' on sounds and make edits or manipulations much more easily at the micro level. And once recording and editing equipment became more portable, this freed electronic artists from the studio, enabling them to compose anywhere.

---

[48] Holmes, 204.

[49] Holmes, 244.

[50] Agostino Di Scipio, 'Granular Synthesis', in *A Xenakis Dictionary*, ed. Dimitris Exarchos (Association Les Amis de Xenakis, 2023), https://www.iannis-xenakis.org/en/granular-synthesis.

Within the pantheon of pop superstars, Icelandic singer Björk was an early adopter of this liberated method of digital music making. In 1999, she began experimenting with a laptop for the first time, opening her up to a new world of sound.[51]

'I recorded all sorts of noises around the house,' she explained. 'I then magnified them up in Pro Tools, and created rhythms with them.' Echoing Xenakis' coinage, she referred to these sounds as 'microbeats' and they became a central element of her 2001 album *Vespertine*. 'It took me like three years,' she said. '[I]t was like crocheting a huge blanket with a tiny needle.'[52]

Björk explained the philosophy of the album in a documentary, appropriately titled *Minuscule*. She compared her 'microbeats' to the microorganisms that invisibly inhabit our physical world. '[I]t sort of gave you a sensation that you've been told a secret,' she said. 'The same way as if you see a picture of a cell in the body magnified very big.'

Just as the world of microorganisms is a complex ecosystem, Björk wanted to mirror this by creating 'a microcosmos of thirty or forty beats' for each song.[53] This sonic bionetwork can be heard clearly on the album's seventh track, 'Aurora'.

The concrete credentials of this song are bolstered further by the participation of electronic duo Matmos. The pair have been vocal about the influence of musique concrète on their

[51] Paul Tingen, 'Inside Track: Björk's Vulnicura', *Sound on Sound*, April 2015, https://www.soundonsound.com/techniques/inside-track-bjorks-vulnicura.
[52] Tingen.
[53] *Minuscule* (2003), [Film] Dir. Ragnheiður Gestsdóttir, Iceland: One Little Indian Records.

work, and even included Xenakis on a 'top ten' list for *Pitchfork* summarizing the genre.[54]

As part of their work on *Vespertine*, Matmos created rhythms from cracked ice[55] and the smacking of Björk's lips.[56] They aren't sounds that are easy to identify and isolate on the finished album. But perhaps that proves Björk's metaphor: just as magnifying in on a cell shows us part of our physical reality that we don't recognize, zooming in on the smallest fragments of sounds defamiliarizes them in such a way that they become transformed.

Maybe the visitors to the Philips Pavilion experienced something like this back in 1958. They would have felt that the ambient crackle of 'Concret PH' was a kind of sound they had never heard before. But they would not have been able to identify its source – nor could they have named its overshadowed composer.

For your recommended listening experience, please pair:

'Concret PH' by Iannis Xenakis, 1958 (2:45)
with
'Aurora' by Björk, 2001 (4:40)

---

[54] Drew Daniel, 'Matmos: Musique Concrète Smash Hits', *Pitchfork*, 30 April 2003, https://pitchfork.com/features/guest-lists/5907-matmos-musique-concrete-smash-hits/.

[55] *Minuscule.*

[56] Matmos, 'When Matmos Met Björk', *Red Bull Music Academy*, 26 June 2013, https://daily.redbullmusicacademy.com/2013/06/when-matmos-met-bjork.

5 Luc Ferrari and the *Groupe de Recherches Musicales*

By the end of the 1950s, peace was breaking out across Europe. Even Pierre Schaeffer, a key belligerent in the conflict between the Paris and Cologne schools of electronic music, admitted that the two sides 'had ended their match in a draw'.[1]

With this thawing in the avant-garde Cold War, opposing forms of electronic music started to blend. New studios appeared, aligned neither to the doctrine of recorded sound favoured by the musique concrète crowd, nor the artificial tone generation of the Germans. One example was Italy's *Studio di Fonologia Musicale* (Studio of Musical Phonology). Here, the directors adopted a specific approach to ensure their 'work should not be directed in a systematic way' – a major contrast to the dogmatic environments of Paris and Cologne.[2]

Another new studio was the UK's BBC Radiophonic Workshop.[3] This experimental unit produced audio effects and

[1] Pierre Schaeffer, *Treatise on Musical Objects: An Essay Across Disciples*, trans. Christine North & John Dack (Berkeley: University of California Press, 2017), 8.
[2] Thom Holmes, *Electronic and Experimental Music: Technology, Music, and Culture*, sixth edition (New York: Routledge, 2020), 254.
[3] Holmes, 348.

music for radio and television, bringing sounds once associated with the avant-garde into millions of ordinary British homes.

The workshop is best remembered for producing the original theme to the sci-fi series *Doctor Who*. Composed by Ron Grainer, the music was realized by Delia Derbyshire using oscillators and tape machine trickery.[4] She had been among the many experimental pilgrims to visit the Philips Pavilion at the 1958 Brussels World's Fair a few years earlier. There she was inspired by Edgard Varèse's *Poème électronique* – a work which seemed to herald this newly liberated era of electronic music making.[5]

The BBC Radiophonic Workshop was also responsible for 'Time Beat', one of the first pop records to directly incorporate musique concrète. The genesis of this piece came from Maddalena Fagandini. She specialized in short compositions played between programmes to let audiences know the station was still broadcasting. One of her works, made with tape loops, caught the ear of producer George Martin.[6] He brought session musicians in to play over it, creating a Latin-flavoured pop single which he put out under the name Ray Cathode. As Martin explained on its release in 1962: 'It is concrete music reinforced by musicians – so we're calling it "reinforced concrete music".'[7]

The single wasn't a great seller. But Martin would reach new commercial heights the next year as the producer for

[4]William L. Weir, *BBC Radiophonic Workshop: A Retrospective* (New York: Bloomsbury Academic, 2023), 50–3.
[5]Weir, 29.
[6]Weir, 35.
[7]Weir, 36.

The Beatles. Through the rest of the decade, Martin and the band would collaborate on increasingly experimental studio recordings, bringing avant-garde innovations to pop charts around the world.

There was nothing quite so commercial on the horizon in Paris. But things were changing there too. Having been 'estranged from the group for three years', Pierre Schaeffer was back at the helm of his *Groupe de Recherches de Musique Concrète* (Research Group for Concrete Music, or GRMC) by 1958.[8] His erstwhile protégé Pierre Henry was on his way out, while a new batch of recruits was coming in. Among their ranks was Iannis Xenakis, the Greek composer and architect who had recently helped design the Philips Pavilion.

The new recruits also included some female composers. Mireille Kyrou was perhaps the most significant, being the only woman to have a commercial record release through the group. Her 'Étude I' (Study I) drew on 'a comb and a feather' as its primary sound sources. It was issued alongside works by Schaeffer and Xenakis on a 1964 compilation simply titled *Musique Concrète*.[9]

Luc Ferrari was another notable recruit. Like Henry, Ferrari had studied at the prestigious Paris Conservatory. But he was too inquisitive for its more conservative instructors. He was allegedly pressured to leave after playing a sonata by modernist composer Béla Bartók in class. 'If you keep on playing this elephant's music, you will never set foot in here again,' his

[8] Olivier Julien, *Musique Concrète: 1956–1962* [CD liner notes], Frémeaux & Associés, 2023.
[9] Axel Kyrou, *Experimental Lineage*, by Mireille Kyrou / Vox Populi! [Digital liner notes], Nostalgie De La Boue, 2019.

teacher told him. And so Ferrari left in search of greater artistic freedom.[10] (Interestingly, Bartók also inspired Halim El-Dabh, the composer of the first-ever work of musique concrète, years earlier when he introduced him to wire recording technology at the Cairo Congress of Arab Music.)

Ferrari soon fell in with the musique concrète crowd, regularly bumping into Schaeffer at galleries and concerts.[11] He even saw Schaeffer and Henry's early performances with their *potentiometre d'espace*, a device that enabled them to pan sounds from speaker to speaker by waving their hands around a set of suspended rings. 'It was mad and disjointed,' Ferrari later recalled. But he 'immediately thought it was a promising direction'.[12]

Schaeffer asked Ferrari to join the GRMC soon after. But the young composer relented for a few years. He summered in Darmstadt in Germany, attending its school for contemporary composers,[13] which counted Karlheinz Stockhausen among its lecturing faculty.[14] After that, Ferrari made a 3-week journey by cargo ship to the United States in search of Edgard Varèse.[15] But by 1958, he was ready to settle down and finally agreed to become part of Schaeffer's group in Paris.[16] Unfortunately, he couldn't have joined at a worse moment.

---

[10] Jacqueline Caux, *Almost Nothing with Luc Ferrari*, trans. Jérôme Hansen (Berlin/Los Angeles: Errant Bodies Press, 2012), 21.

[11] Caux, 26.

[12] Caux, 24.

[13] Caux, 26.

[14] *Encyclopedia Britannica*, 'Karlheinz Stockhausen', 18 August 2024, https://www.britannica.com/biography/Karlheinz-Stockhausen.

[15] Caux, 139.

[16] Caux, 12.

Ferrari started as an assistant to Pierre Henry. He found his new boss '[m]ore intimidating than Pierre Schaeffer [. . .] more secretive, more silent'. The reason for this behaviour quickly became evident, as Henry made a dramatic exit from the GRMC shortly after Ferrari's arrival. 'I had noticed when attending the meetings that things weren't going well,' Ferrari later recalled, referring to the fracturing relationship between the two Pierres. At one meeting, Ferrari witnessed Henry handing in his resignation: 'He didn't give Schaeffer the letter so much as throw it in his direction – and it was a big letter!'[17]

Although Henry took 'his entire team' with him, the new-joiner Ferrari was left behind. As the primary composer for the GRMC, Henry's absence created a void. So, Ferrari, 'a novice in experimental music', had to learn to handle the tape machines quickly to support the GRMC's continued output.[18]

One of Ferrari's first musique concrète works was the 3-minute 'Étude aux sons tendus' (Study of stretched sounds). 'The idea was to use sounds like you would use an elastic band,' Ferrari explained.[19] The piece had its premiere at the 1958 Brussels World's Fair. Ferrari later suggested that he found this early work 'very clumsy'.[20] But it nonetheless opened up a new language of composition for him, offering a creative freedom that had been denied at the Paris Conservatory. Ferrari felt a sense of optimism while in Brussels too. 'There was a beautiful moment of effervescence,' he recalled, noting the

[17] Caux, 27.

[18] Caux, 27.

[19] Luc Ferrari, 'Étude aux sons tendus', *Maison ONA*, https://maison-ona.com/catalog-0306ONA.

[20] Ferrari, 'Étude aux sons tendus.'

presence of his former lecturer, Stockhausen, as well as proto-concrete pioneer John Cage. 'It was a time of great friendship.'[21]

But back in Paris, things were less harmonious. Pierre Schaeffer had renamed his unit the *Groupe de Recherches Musicales* (Musical Research Group, or GRM). This new title suggested a widening of scope and a withdrawal of the musique concrète term. But at the same time, Schaeffer was formulating an ambitious music theory, which seemed to reinforce his dogma on what sounds were permissible in electronic music. 'Things deteriorated as soon as Pierre Schaeffer started working on his *solfege* [music theory],' Ferrari alleged. '[H]e was paying less and less attention to the work of composers, and more and more to the individual work he wanted to do.'[22]

Schaffer's relationships with the GRM's key figures began to deteriorate. One of his longest-standing partners was Pierre Boulez. He had been there from the beginning, recording the piano sounds for Schaeffer's landmark *Cinq études de bruits* (Five Studies of Noises) in 1948.[23] But now, more than a decade later, their relationship had 'turned violent'. As Ferrari remembered, 'Boulez left the Studio furious and fell out with Schaeffer and musique concrète forever.'[24]

Tensions were equally high with the surly Greek, Iannis Xenakis. When the idea of a group concert was raised, Xenakis presented some initial ideas. Schaeffer rejected these and

[21] Caux, 28.
[22] Caux, 29.
[23] James Nice, *The French Avant-Garde in the 20th Century* [CD liner notes], LTM Recordings, 2014.
[24] Caux, 30.

Xenakis immediately left the project.[25] Soon after, he quit the GRM entirely. 'I don't know why, but he blamed me,' Ferrari recalled. 'I felt terribly sad, because I didn't understand.'[26]

Part of this blame might have come from Ferrari's role as 'a kind of psychological shock absorber'. He positioned himself between the increasingly abrasive Schaeffer and his aggrieved colleagues. 'There were all these tensions going on,' Ferrari later explained. 'I was always in Schaeffer's office trying to work things out.'[27]

But despite his position as the office diplomat, Ferrari had his own rebellious streak. 'I was a deviant,' he said.[28] That quality expressed itself as far back as his days at the Paris Conservatory, when he thrust Bartók's 'elephant's music' into the unsuspecting ears of his teacher. And now, it would emerge again as he embarked on his most ambitious work for the GRM: the 1964 composition *Hétérozygote*.

Years earlier, Henry had rebelled against Schaeffer's doctrine by using artificial tones. Now, Ferrari would leave his mentor's dogma by incorporating recorded sounds that had not been manipulated. Across the 20-minute *Hétérozygote*, Ferrari included clearly audible spoken word passages, the splashing of water, and the bleating of sheep. By keeping these sounds recognizable, he proposed to inaugurate a new genre, which he dubbed 'anecdotal music'.

In Ferrari's definition, the anecdotal genre combined 'musical' sounds with 'dramatic' sounds, so that 'various interpretations

[25] Caux, 37.
[26] Caux, 41.
[27] Caux, 41.
[28] Caux, 33.

may arise' for the listener. In other words, Ferrari's project was no longer about the pure manipulation of sound. It was about using recognizable noises to suggest a kind of story, inviting the listener 'to imagine his own anecdote'.[29]

This music departed from Schaeffer's vision. However, Ferrari believed his mentor would appreciate what he was trying to achieve. 'I was naïve,' Ferrari admitted later. 'I thought he would like it.' Needless to say, Schaeffer did not like it. 'I was surprised by his reaction, by his violence,' Ferrari recalled. 'He said it was incoherent, formless, that it was noise. It shocked me deeply'.[30]

Despite incurring Schaeffer's wrath, Ferrari remained with the GRM. But he began to distance himself from the rest of the group. He shifted his attention to projects outside the realm of musique concrète composition. Notably, he directed a series of documentaries on musicians. One followed his old lecturer, Stockhausen, as he rehearsed an orchestra.[31] Another memorialized Edgard Varèse, who Ferrari had once sailed across the Atlantic to visit. By this time, Varèse seemed to have become something of a unifying figure among the electronic avant-garde community. Despite their feuds, Pierre Schaeffer, Pierre Boulez and Iannis Xenakis all participated in the documentary.[32]

---

[29] Luc Ferrari, 'Hétérozygote', *Maison ONA*, https://maison-ona.com/catalog-0084ONA.

[30] Caux, 34.

[31] *Luc Ferrari Catalog*, 1966, http://lucferrari.com/en/catalogue/1966-2/.

[32] 'The Great Rehearsals: Hommage to Edgard Varèse', *Close-Up Film Centre* [film description], 2019, https://www.closeupfilmcentre.com/film_programmes/2019/luc-ferrari/hommage-to-edgard-varese/.

Even so, in 1966 Ferrari left the GRM.[33] With his newfound freedom, he returned to the idea of anecdotal music. He recorded the sounds of village life during a stay on the island of Korčula in Yugoslavia.[34] He carefully assembled these recordings into a 'sonic photographic slide' representing a 'most faithful and realistic reminiscence possible of a fishing village at dawn.'[35] In this way, Ferrari took his idea of anecdotal music further than he had with *Hétérozygote*. With this new piece, he fully abandoned the concept of sonic manipulation on which musique concrète was founded. Instead, he assembled a collage of entirely recognisable sounds to capture the essence of a specific time and place.

Ferrari titled his piece *Presque Rien n°1* (Almost Nothing n°1), suggesting an alignment with minimalism. But his work more closely prefigured the genre of soundscapes, which became hugely popular from the 1970s on. (Think of those recordings of rainforest sounds or ocean waves, which are so ubiquitous in New Age outlets.)

Ferrari followed his first *Presque Rien* with several sequels. But he also explored other kinds of music. 'I had more time on my hands,' Ferrari explained. 'In the early 1970s, I went in search of different musical genres. I worked with people who came from rock, folk and chanson.'[36]

Jacqueline Caux, who published a book of interviews with Ferrari, went so far as to claim that he took part in 'all

[33] Caux, 12.
[34] Luc Ferrari, *Presque Rien n°1: Le lever du jour au bord de la mer*, trans. Edward J. P. Williams (Paris: Maison ONA, 2018), 6.
[35] Ferrari, *Presque Rien n°1*, 4.
[36] Caux, 50.

the musical ideologies of the second half of the twentieth century'.[37] That may sound like hyperbole. But Ferrari's output reflects a remarkable diversity. His catalogue contains about 150 pieces.[38] As well as his musique concrète and anecdotal music, he also composed for full orchestra,[39] solo piano,[40] saxophone quartet,[41] and even one piece for 'a soloist singer who is accompanied by a tambourine'.[42] Ferrari seems to have made a point of ensuring he was always surrounded by 'a mixed group of people,' including those 'from jazz, contemporary music, chanson', and more.[43]

Ferrari had an intriguing theory that might explain why he felt this inexhaustible drive to experiment with different genres. He argued that 'a capitalist society' requires constant 'renewal', so it is 'necessary to replace the objects to be consumed at a faster and faster rate'. These objects not only include physical goods, he added, but also music and culture: hence, Ferrari concluded, 'the race for innovation and the birth of the concept of the avant-garde'.[44]

Ferrari's conclusion feels counterintuitive at first. After all, there are few kinds of music less commercial than musique concrète. But perhaps the avant-garde is commercial in a different way. It might be seen as a kind of factory of ideas

---

[37] Caux, 9.

[38] Luc Ferrari, *Maison ONA,* https://maison-ona.com/composer-Ferrari.

[39] *Luc Ferrari Catalog*, 1967, http://lucferrari.com/en/catalogue/1967-2/.

[40] *Luc Ferrari Catalog*, 1952, http://lucferrari.com/en/catalogue/1952-2/.

[41] *Luc Ferrari Catalog*, 1978, http://lucferrari.com/en/catalogue/1978-2/.

[42] *Luc Ferrari Catalog*, 1970, http://lucferrari.com/en/catalogue/1970-2/.

[43] Caux, 51.

[44] Luc Ferrari, 'Originality and Consumerism Society', in *Preface to . . . and thoughts on . . .*, by Luc Ferrari, trans. Edward J. P. Williams (Paris: Maison ONA, 2021), 5.

– a laboratory for cultural experimentation. Most of its weird outputs will fade into obscurity. But occasionally an idea will take off and enter the mainstream world of cultural commerce.

This would become increasingly evident through the 1960s and 1970s, as techniques originated by musique concrète pioneers became mainstays of pop music, blockbuster movie sound effects, and even advertising. This absorption of the avant-garde into popular culture created many of the great artworks of the twentieth century. But the process that enabled it was, in Ferrari's estimation, a 'barbaric and systematic exploitation'.[45]

So while the 1958 Brussels World's Fair promised a new utopia for electronic musicians, it actually delivered a world as imperfect as the last. True, the Cold War of the Paris and Cologne schools had ended peacefully. But what was that worth when civil war at the GRM continued to rage? Likewise, there were new opportunities for artistic freedom and collaboration across borders. But, as Ferrari suggested, in a globalized world where ideas are endlessly consumed, the individual innovators who generate them are 'relegated to the margins of society'.[46]

'The contemporary Western world consumes originality,' Ferrari wearily concluded.[47] And, as some practitioners of musique concrète would soon find out, the people manufacturing such originality might find themselves consumed too.

---

[45] Ferrari, 'Originality and Consumerism Society', 5.
[46] Ferrari, 'Originality and Consumerism Society', 5.
[47] Ferrari, 'Originality and Consumerism Society', 5.

A concrete pairing: Luc Ferrari and Brian Eno

If you'd just spent 8 years with Pierre Schaeffer and his *Groupe de Recherches Musicales*, you might need a holiday too. So, it was no surprise to find Luc Ferrari in the Dalmatian Islands the summer after his departure.[48] He had been invited by friends to stay in a fishing village on the island of Korčula. While most visitors focused on sun and sea, Ferrari was fixated by the local sounds. 'From our room we could see the little fishing port nestled between the hills, which gave it an extraordinary acoustic quality,' Ferrari recalled. 'So I left the microphone on the windowsill and, every night from 4am to 6am, I recorded.'[49]

Ferrari captured the ordinary noises of a village coming to life at dawn: the buzz of insects, a cart trundling along, roosters crowing and locals chatting. Most exciting to Ferrari was the sound of motorboats, whose 'echoes reveal the shape of the mountains around the harbor.'[50]

Over the following years, Ferrari edited these recordings into a 20-minute composition. He called it *Presque Rien n°1 ou Le lever du jour au bord de la mer* (Almost Nothing n°1 or Sunrise by the Sea). 'I composed by means of the most undetectable interventions,' he said, indicating that the sounds themselves were unmanipulated – they were simply ordered and structured to create a sonic narrative in a condensed time frame.[51]

[48] Ferrari, *Presque Rien n°1*, 6.
[49] Ferrari, *Presque Rien n°1*, 6.
[50] Caux, 109.
[51] Ferrari, *Presque Rien n°1*, 6.

Ferrari returned to this mode of composing, which he called 'anecdotal music', through the rest of his career. 'I was making sound films that you could only see in the mind's eye,' Ferrari explained. 'I believe I was the first composer to use these "found objects" in the music world.'[52]

But despite Ferrari's claim to being first, a similar project was going on simultaneously in the United States. A young New Yorker, Irv Teibel, had discovered the power of environmental sound while helping a friend record ocean waves for a film.[53] When working on the tape in the editing room, Teibel noticed the sounds made him feel relaxed.[54] Soon, he realized this might have commercial potential.

Teibel released his ocean wave sounds in 1969. The album, *environments*, became a surprise hit and was picked up by Atlantic Records.[55] Through the rest of the 1970s, Teibel released ten more albums, constructing soundscapes from the creaking of a wooden sailboat, the birdsong of an English meadow, and the trickling of rain in a pine forest. Some of Teibel's compositions even followed a narrative like Ferrari's *Presque Rien* – particularly his recordings of 'Dawn at New Hope, PA' and 'Dawn in the Okefenokee Swamp.'[56]

---

[52] Caux, 130.

[53] 'About Irv Teibel', *Irv Teibel Archive*, https://www.irvteibel.com/irv-teibel/.

[54] Mike Powell, 'Natural Selection: How a New Age Hustler Sold the Sound of the World', *Pitchfork*, 2 November 2016, https://pitchfork.com/features/cover-story/9971-natural-selection-how-a-new-age-hustler-sold-the-sound-of-the-world/.

[55] 'environments 1', *Irv Teibel Archive*, https://www.irvteibel.com/discography/environments/.

[56] 'Catalog', *Irv Teibel Archive*, https://www.irvteibel.com/catalog/.

But while Ferrari's work was a product of the avant-garde, Teibel marketed his recordings to a mass audience. Catalogue advertisements boasted that the records 'can be used for relaxation, meditation, alpha inducement, self-hypnosis, concentration, sex and virtually any application'.[57] These myriad suggestions for how Teibel's sounds might be 'used' opened up a new way of listening for consumers. But it wasn't exactly music. Indeed, the tagline for Teibel's albums declared: 'The Music of the Future Isn't Music.'[58]

A few years after the release of Ferrari's *Presque Rien* and Teibel's soundscapes, this new way of listening found a more musical expression through the 'ambient' genre. Brian Eno coined this term for his 1978 album *Ambient 1: Music for Airports*. In the liner notes, Eno explained his vision. Ambient music should 'induce calm and a space to think', he declared. It should also enhance the 'acoustic and atmospheric idiosyncrasies' of a particular environment.[59]

Eno's subsequent ambient albums focused on more precise environments, paralleling Ferrari and Teibel's compositions. On *Ambient 4: On Land*, Eno's final track, 'Dunwich Beach, Autumn, 1960', is particularly precise: pinpointing a location, season and year. Its quiet, echoey instrumentation certainly suggests a cold desolation reminiscent of an English seaside village in the darkening part of the year. But unlike Ferrari and Teibel's works, which generate associations entirely through sound,

---

[57]'Syntonic Images', *Irv Teibel Archive*, https://www.irvteibel.com/galleries/syntonic-images/.

[58]'Syntonic Images.'

[59]Brian Eno, *Ambient 1: Music for Airports* [CD liner notes], Virgin Records, 2009.

Eno's more abstract composition requires a descriptive title to conjure an image in the listener's mind.

Still, one can trace an evolution from musique concrète, to anecdotal music, to soundscapes, to ambient music. But the exact links between each stage are harder to prove. For instance, we know Irv Teibel was an amateur practitioner of musique concrète.[60] But he could not have been influenced directly by Ferrari's *Presque Rien* – even though that work was started in 1967, before Teibel recorded his waves, it was only completed in 1970, after Teibel's album had been released.[61]

So, while there is a thread to be followed across these interrelated genres, it's likely that they emerged as a kind of parallel evolution. Once recording technologies improved and became portable, it was suddenly possible to capture environmental sounds and edit them into coherent compositions. Thus, simultaneous ideas of how to wield and build on this ability emerged continents apart. Some of these ideas held clear similarities. But they were different enough to gradually evolve into new kinds of sound art or music.

For your recommended listening experience, please pair:

'Presque Rien n°1' by Luc Ferrari, 1970 (20:46)
with
'Dunwich Beach, Autumn, 1960' by Brian Eno, 1982 (7:13)

[60] Powell.
[61] *Luc Ferrari Catalog*, 1970, http://lucferrari.com/en/catalogue/1970-2/.

6 Tod Dockstader and the sound hobbyists

In Europe, national studios dedicated to electronic music sprang up throughout the 1950s. France and Germany had their publicly funded studios in Paris and Cologne. The UK had its BBC Radiophonic Workshop. But in America, there was no such centralized approach. The United States had to make do with a scattering of small experimental hubs across its vast continental breadth. And many were shoestring operations.

When the Columbia Tape Music Center was founded in 1952, it had no studio at all. It simply consisted of a bunch of portable equipment that had to be shifted from one place to another by car.[1] Despite its name, the Cooperative Studio for Electronic Music in Michigan had no studio either. Instead, the equipment was divided between each of the co-founders' homes.[2] At least the San Francisco Tape Music Center had a site of its own when it launched in 1961. But this was in a condemned building.[3]

Gradually, some of these modest enterprises gained traction. The Columbia Tape Music Center eventually evolved into the Columbia-Princeton Electronic Music Center with

[1]Thom Holmes, *Electronic and Experimental Music: Technology, Music, and Culture*, sixth edition (New York: Routledge, 2020), 287.
[2]Holmes, *Electronic and Experimental Music*, 309.
[3]Holmes, *Electronic and Experimental Music*, 326.

the help of a Rockefeller grant.[4] Once that facility opened, notable composers like Halim El-Dabh moved in. The eccentric Egyptian, who unwittingly inaugurated the musique concrète genre in 1944, had been living in the United States for a decade by that point. With the equipment at the Columbia-Princeton studio, he could return to his experimental roots, playing with tape loops 'that were so long that they had to be run out of the room and back.'[5]

But even as some of these experimental studios grew in funding and esteem, the American approach to electronic music remained more individualistic than the European project. There was no national theory – no equivalent to the French model of manipulating recorded sound, or the German model of artificial tone generation. Instead, there was something of a 'free for all', allowing diverse styles to emerge, unfettered by the constraints of any centralized rulebook.

The increasing availability of wire recorders and tape machines through both military surplus and the mass market bolstered the American project. This enabled amateur sound hobbyists to conduct experiments at home. Many notable American sound artists began their careers this way.

One of the youngest was Walter Murch. Though he would later find fame as the Oscar-winning sound designer for films like *Apocalypse Now* and *The English Patient*, his audio experiments began as a child in the 1950s. Working with a home tape recorder, the pre-teen Murch created his own 'collages of sounds, naturally recorded sounds, put in different

[4] Holmes, *Electronic and Experimental Music*, 295.
[5] Holmes, *Electronic and Experimental Music*, 305.

orders."[6] When he chanced upon a radio broadcast of Pierre Schaeffer and Pierre Henry's work, he realized there was a name for the weird compositions he had been constructing – musique concrète.

'Suddenly, I had this realization that the world is much bigger than I thought,' Murch recalled. His epiphany seemed to recognize the convergent evolution that was taking place in electronic music, as the same ideas were developed independently in different corners of the globe.[7] Just as Halim El-Dabh had stumbled upon musique concrète separately to Pierre Schaeffer, Murch discovered this strange new mode of composition in isolation too. But the convergent evolution was happening *within* the United States as well. As music historian Thom Holmes describes it, the development of American electronic music was 'largely an explosion of parallel activities [. . .] all happening at the same time.'[8]

On the other side of the country from Murch's New York experimentation, musique concrète was also popping up in California. In San Francisco in 1959, Pauline Oliveros completed her first composition, called 'Time Perspectives.' Her work was also constructed with the amateur tools of the sound hobbyist – in her case, a Sears and Roebuck home tape recorder. Using just the sounds of her voice, two soup ladles, and a table knife, she created a 20-minute work of remarkable

[6]Web of Stories, 'What is musique concrète?' [video interview with Walter Murch], https://www.webofstories.com/play/walter.murch/12.
[7]Web of Stories.
[8]Thom Holmes, 'Crosscurrents in Electronic Tape Music in the United States,' *ThomHolmes.com*, 19 June 2023, https://www.thomholmes.com/post/crosscurrents-in-electronic-tape-music-in-the-united-states.

sonic sophistication. Lacking any professional equipment for sound manipulation, she placed cardboard tubes over the microphone to create a low-budget filter and used her bathtub as a reverberation chamber.[9]

The convergent evolution was also found in America's heartland. In Minnesota, Tod Dockstader spent his childhood building ham radios out of empty Quaker Oats cannisters. In his high school years, he started composing on steel wire, using an old military recorder. Like all sound hobbyists of the time, Dockstader improvised with his tools, using the tip of a lit cigarette to make cuts in the wire. 'You had to tie the wire, which was very fine, in a perfect square knot,' he remembered years later, describing the painstaking process of editing cut wire back together.[10]

But once Dockstader graduated from college, he gained a significant advantage over most other sound hobbyists in America. Finding his way into the film industry, he became an editor, writer and storyboard artist for animated productions. This gave him access to equipment and recording studios that were unavailable to most of the population. And with these tools, he took his work to the next level.

By day, Dockstader worked on his cartoons, cutting sound and picture for *Mister Magoo* and *The Gerald McBoing-Boing Show*.[11] He even wrote an episode of *Tom and Jerry*, a

---

[9]Pauline Oliveros, *Four Electronic Pieces 1959–1966* [CD liner notes], Sub Rosa, 2008.

[10]Geeta Dayal, 'Legends of Electronic Music: Tod Dockstader', *Wired*, 7 June 2012, https://www.wired.com/2012/06/tod-dockstader/.

[11]Tom Steenland, 'Remembering Tod Dockstader (1932–2015)', *New Music USA*, 27 March 2015, https://newmusicusa.org/nmbx/remembering-tod-dockstader-1932-2015/.

particularly oddball instalment which sees the titular rodent enlist as an 'astro-mouse' to escape his feline pursuer.[12] But after dark, Dockstader snuck back into the studio to work on his musique concrète compositions. 'I was always working at night – deep night,' Dockstader recalled. 'And I'd be very careful. If they found me in a studio – just me – I would have lost my job.'[13]

At the time, it's unlikely Dockstader would have referred to his compositions as musique concrète. He was still working in that isolated state of convergent evolution common to the American sound hobbyist. 'I don't think I modeled my first work after anyone,' he said. 'I just knew how to do it.'[14] Later, Dockstader became aware of a kindred spirit in Edgard Varèse, the wild-haired old composer whose *Poème électronique* had reached over a million listeners at the 1958 Brussels World's Fair. When Dockstader heard that composition, it struck him as 'a powerfully dramatic work'. He even adopted Varèse's term 'organized sound' to describe his own compositions. And he drew strength from Varèse's steadfast attitude in the face of ridicule. To Varèse, electronic music 'wasn't a joke or a momentary blip', Dockstader noted. 'That attitude sustained me in my own work.'[15]

It was appropriate that Dockstader's breakthrough came when he shared a radio spot with Varèse in 1961.[16] The piece

[12] *Mouse Into Space* (1962), [Short film] Dir. Gene Deitch, United States & Czechoslovakia: Metro-Goldwyn-Mayer (MGM).
[13] Dayal.
[14] Steenland.
[15] Steenland.
[16] Steenland.

selected was a world premiere, the finale of his first record, *Eight Electronic Pieces*. Dockstader described the track as 'in effect, my *Poème électronique*'.[17] So, it should have been a thrill to share the billing with the composer of the original. But the broadcast turned into a shambles.

As Dockstader later recounted, the station engineer 'treated it as an add-a-part composition', playing his own noises over the top of Dockstader's work using a test-tone generator. 'I thought I was going crazy,' Dockstader recalled. 'But, it was typical of the reaction at that time: this isn't Music, it's a joke, let's have some fun with it.'[18]

The station engineer added 'some boops and beeps of his own' over Varèse's piece too. But the elder composer seemed to react with grace, perhaps hardened by the dreadful reaction to his piece *Déserts* in 1954. After the broadcast, he called Dockstader to simply say how nice it was for their works to be paired together on air. He even suggested they collaborate in the future.[19]

Unfortunately, such a joint project never materialized; the elderly Varèse died just a few years later. But a torch was being passed: as Varèse's career and life were winding down, the young Dockstader entered his most prolific phase, which would see him produce a remarkable volume of diverse works over the next 5 years.

Although unconstrained by any rulebook for electronic music composition, Dockstader largely focused on the

[17] 'Tod Dockstader: Apocalypse,' Starkland catalog, https://starkland.org/catalog/st202/.
[18] Steenland.
[19] Steenland.

concrete approach of manipulating found sounds. There was no theory behind this. For Dockstader, it was a financial matter. 'I didn't have the money for electronic sounds,' he recalled years later. 'I had to have things like bottles, or anything that would make a noise. It didn't matter what it was; if it sounded interesting, or I could make it interesting, I'd go for it.'[20]

One of the most impressive examples was his 1963 composition *Water Music*. He made this six-part work from manipulated recordings of dripping water. Each section of the piece had a distinct sound that was designed to reflect a different aquatic quality. Among the 'instruments' listed in the liner notes, Dockstader included 'two water glasses, a Coke bottle, [and] a metal garbage can (to hold the water)'.[21]

Water Music is also noteworthy for demonstrating another example of convergent evolution in the world of musique concrète. A few years earlier, a Canadian sound engineer, Hugh Le Caine, had created his own composition made entirely from the sound of falling water drops. Although he didn't consider himself a composer, Le Caine's 2-minute 'Dripsody' became one of the most famous works of musique concrète. As music historian Thom Holmes recalls: 'For many years, *Dripsody* was undoubtedly the most often played tape composition in any college music course.'[22]

But while Le Caine's 'Dripsody' became a favourite in academic circles, Dockstader's *Water Music* seemed destined for wider success. In June 1963, New York's WQXR radio station

[20] Dayal.
[21] Dayal.
[22] Holmes, *Electronic and Experimental Music*, 340.

selected it for broadcast. This time, Dockstader's premiere was paired with a work by Karlheinz Stockhausen, the German composer who had started out at Pierre Schaeffer's studio in 1952. Unfortunately, the broadcast ended up being even more disastrous than the last. As the programme finished, the unimpressed host announced that electronic music clearly had no future, and vowed that such a broadcast would never happen again.[23]

But even if Dockstader disagreed with the host's verdict, he was beginning to understand that his type of electronic music was dying out. In 1964, he received an invitation to see an early demonstration of a Moog synthesiser. This device enabled a huge variety of artificial sounds to be played on a keyboard, enabling composers without engineering skills to make sophisticated electronic music for the first time. 'I listened, and I got a sinking feeling that my kind of music was ending here,' Dockstader recalled. 'My peculiar skills were going to be obsolete, like a blacksmith looking at his first automobile. That [Moog] keyboard: that meant the writers were going to take over electronic music.'[24]

Despite this, Dockstader persisted for a couple more years. His efforts culminated in the album *Quatermass*, which has been described as 'Dockstader's tour de force'[25] and 'his masterpiece'.[26] The five-part composition has a darker, more

---

[23] Steenland.

[24] Steenland.

[25] John Bush, '*Quatermass* review', *AllMusic*, https://www.allmusic.com/album/quatermass-mw0000939628.

[26] Jason Ankeny, 'Tod Dockstader Biography', *AllMusic*, https://www.allmusic.com/artist/tod-dockstader-mn0000510645#biography.

menacing tone than earlier works like *Water Music*. It also draws on a wider variety of sound sources, including gongs, a roll of adhesive tape, and white noise from the radio. But the central sound on the album came from a simple red balloon. 'It's one balloon – overdubbed – multiplied – into a choir,' Dockstader explained. '[I]t's a child's trick: you blow up a balloon and then you hold the neck of it and you let the air out very slowly, and by stretching the neck or releasing it you can change the pitch of it – it becomes a double-reed instrument.'[27]

But for all Dockstader's ingenuity in transforming ordinary sounds into alien forms on *Quatermass*, the avant-garde album was never going to be a hit. It had a small listing in *Billboard* magazine under the 'new releases' section[28] and seems to have attracted only one review: in *Audio*, a magazine for technicians and audiophiles. Though this was a positive notice, it included several backhanded compliments. The review begins by describing Dockstader as 'an outsider and a loner' who 'is technically "illiterate" from the inside musical viewpoint.' But the writer goes on to say that Dockstader, for all his sound hobbyist origins, has 'more sense of music in him than many of the Chosen who do have access to the fancy equipment.'[29]

Despite this glimmer of promise, Dockstader's career as a composer was effectively over by the time the review was published. He had left his job in animation to work on the Air Canada Pavilion for the 1967 Montreal World's Fair. With this move, he lost access to the studio equipment needed

[27] Tod Dockstader, *Quatermass* [LP liner notes], Owl Records, 1966.
[28] *Billboard*, 2 July 1966, 46.
[29] Edward Tatnall Canby, 'Record Revue', *Audio*, August, 1966, 86.

to produce his 'organized sound'. He applied for grants from institutions like the Columbia-Princeton Electronic Music Center (where Halim El-Dabh had enjoyed a few years of experimentation). But he was rejected for having insufficient academic qualifications.[30]

In any case, Dockstader's priorities were changing. He and his wife had a daughter to care for, and that took precedence over unprofitable sonic experimentation. 'I just got bone-tired,' Dockstader reflected years later. 'I'd almost lived in that studio for six, seven years, engineering by day and doing my music in down-time, nights, and weekends there. *Concrète* and electronic music was an expensive music to make, then; it cost a lot in time and money.'[31]

But Dockstader's retirement allowed the torch to be passed again. The year he left the music scene also saw the release of *Freak Out!*, the debut album from California rock band The Mothers of Invention. One of the keystones of experimental rock, this double album concluded with two tracks that incorporated elements of musique concrète. These included cut-and-paste techniques to create a kind of studio jam collage, as well as sped-up tape playback.[32]

Frank Zappa, the creative force behind the album, was aware of Dockstader's work. 'He was more of an engineer than a composer,' Zappa remembered in a later interview. '[T]o me

---

30 Steenland.

31 Steenland.

32 François Couture, 'The Return of the Son of Monster Magnet Review', *AllMusic*, https://www.allmusic.com/song/the-return-of-the-son-of-monster-magnet-mt0044284071.

some of [Dockstader's] compositions work better than the supposedly serious big shots from Europe,' he added.[33]

Zappa also shared Dockstader's love for Varèse. He even gave one of the tracks on *Freak Out!* the subtitle 'In Memoriam, Edgard Varèse'. This admiration for the elderly composer began in Zappa's childhood. For his fifteenth birthday, he had requested that his mother spent her five-dollar gift budget on a long-distance phone call so he could speak to Varèse in New York.[34]

Now, Dockstader was inspiring a new generation of rock stars too. The British blues band Ten Years After cited him as an influence on their 1969 album *Stonedhenge*, which was released a few months before their legendary appearance at Woodstock. 'There's quite a lot of Todd [*sic*] Dockstader in there,' band leader Alvin Lee said. 'I was into my musique concrete [sic] phase,' he clarified, implying that purloining avant-garde innovations had become an archetypal stepping stone of any rockstar's journey by that point.[35]

Later that year, music from Dockstader's first album, *Eight Electronic Pieces*, was featured in the film *Satyricon*.[36] Directed by Federico Fellini, this Roman fantasy of hedonistic excess found an audience on the arthouse circuit, was nominated for an Oscar, and even entered the public lexicon. When John

[33] John Diliberto, 'Frank Zappa and His Digital Orchestra', *Electronic Musician*, September 1986, 52.
[34] Frank Zappa & Peter Occhiogrosso, *The Real Frank Zappa Book* (New York: Poseidon Press, 1989), 33.
[35] Hugh Fielder, 'The Troubled Tale of Ten Years After: from Woodstock to the World', *Classic Rock*, 22 January 2020, https://www.loudersound.com/features/the-story-of-ten-years-after-from-woodstock-to-the-world.
[36] Dayal.

Lennon described the debauchery of his early tours with The Beatles in *Rolling Stone*, he noted: 'They were Satyricon, all right.'[37]

But even as his 'organized sound' was permeating into the popular culture, Dockstader remained out of the spotlight. Being an avant-garde innovator doesn't always pay the bills, and he wouldn't return to composing until the 2000s. Still, during those decades of artistic inactivity Dockstader's influence broadened as subsequent generations passed on his musique concrète spirit second- and third-hand. His name was rarely acknowledged. But his influence was there – in the sounds.

A concrete pairing: Tod Dockstader and The Who

Once you start thinking about the influence of musique concrète, you can begin to believe it's everywhere. Maybe it's in Jimi Hendrix's backwards guitar on 'Castles Made of Sand'? Perhaps it's in the instrumental loops that form the foundation of hip-hop? You could even argue it's in any music that incorporates recorded sound – from the rainfall on 'Riders on the Storm' by The Doors, to the gunshots on M.I.A's 'Paper Planes'.

[37] Jann Wenner, 'The Rolling Stone Interview: John Lennon, Part One: The Working Class Hero', *Rolling Stone*, 21 January 1971, https://www.johnlennon.com/music/interviews/rolling-stone-interview-1970/.

But while it's easy to suggest these connections, it's much harder to substantiate a direct line of inspiration. Most of the influence of musique concrète trickled into the mainstream through second- or third-hand channels. But occasionally, we can trace a direct point of contact. And so it is with Tod Dockstader, who in 1969 had his 'organized sound' incorporated into one of the cornerstones of classic rock.

The work in question is *Tommy* by The Who – one of the first 'rock operas' ever produced (and certainly the most famous). Conceived and composed by the band's guitarist, Pete Townshend, the album tells the story of a 'deaf, dumb and blind boy'. Living on a higher sensory plane, the title character experiences strange 'musical dreams', and eventually becomes a spiritual guru.[38]

Before recording with his band, Townshend created a solo demo of the album. To reflect the strangeness of Tommy's 'musical dreams', he incorporated excerpts from Dockstader's recordings as placeholders. These were moments where Townshend was essentially leaving a note for himself to say, 'I want to do something like this here'. When the album was recorded in the studio, the band created their own sound effects and replaced the Dockstader originals.[39]

Since Dockstader's music didn't directly feature on the final album, he was not credited. And his influence on *Tommy* was

---

[38] 'Amazing Journey' (1969), [Song] written by Pete Townshend, performed by The Who, Track Record/Polydor Records Ltd.

[39] Justin H. Brierley, 'An Exciting email, and a Reflection on musique concrète in Everyday Life', *Unlocking Dockstader* [Blog], 16 June 2013, https://unlockingdockstader.blogspot.com/2013/06/an-exciting-email-and-reflection-on.html.

not known until 2013, when Townshend decided to release a 'super deluxe' version of the album, including his original demos. As Dockstader documentarian Justin H. Brierley recalls, Townshend 'went searching for Tod in order to properly credit him'.[40]

Dockstader was living with dementia by this time and would pass away a couple of years later.[41] But Townshend contacted the composer's daughter. Together, they arranged for Dockstader to receive a credit on the new edition of the album, bringing his unknown contribution to a rock classic to light for the first time in over 40 years.

On the original release of the album, that long-hidden influence can be detected on the 'reverse guitar and swannee whistle'[42] effects on tracks like 'Amazing Journey'. Some of those sounds pair well with Dockstader's *Water Music*, a six-part composition demonstrating a remarkable sonic diversity sourced from 'sewers, kitchen sinks, toilets and other unlikely places'.[43]

Compared to Dockstader's musique concrète, Townshend felt that his own 'nonsense' sound effects might 'disappoint serious scholars' of the genre.[44] But the impurity of his concrete imitation is not important. What matters is the simple acknowledgement that Dockstader's work had a direct impact on one of the most popular creators of rock music of the time.

---

[40] Brierley [Blog].

[41] *Unlocking Dockstader* (2012), [Short film] Dir. Justin H. Brierley, https://vimeo.com/41200802.

[42] Brierley [Blog].

[43] Dayal.

[44] Brierley [Blog].

Given that it took more than 40 years for this particular influence to be revealed, there are likely many more instances of major artists taking first-hand inspiration from Tod Dockstader and the concrete crowd. If we draw that influence down to its second and third generations and beyond, it might expand into infinity, like the branches of an enormous, overlapping family tree. So, perhaps they are justified – those who hear the influence of musique concrète everywhere.

For your recommended listening experience, please pair:

'Water Music, Pt. Two' by Tod Dockstader, 1963 (2:56)
with
'Amazing Journey' by The Who, 1969 (5:04)

7 Karlheinz Stockhausen and mainstreaming the avant-garde

By the mid-1960s, musique concrète was seeping into the mainstream of rock and pop, thanks to influences like Edgard Varèse and Tod Dockstader. But the greatest conduit for connecting avant-garde and popular music was Karlheinz Stockhausen.

The German had come a long way since his early days with Pierre Schaeffer in 1952. Back then, his studio time had been so limited that he continued cutting tape at night in his hostel. With no way to hear the results, it was tedious work. 'I can no longer recall exactly how many weeks I carried on this cutting and splicing,' he later said.[1]

But Stockhausen's dedication paid off. The following year, he began lecturing at the famous Darmstadt School, which counted Luc Ferrari among its attendees.[2] When Varèse's infamous composition *Déserts* premiered the year after,

[1] Karlheinz Stockhausen, *Elektronische Musik 1952–1960* [CD liner notes], Stockhausen-Verlag, 1991.

[2] *Encyclopedia Britannica*, 'Karlheinz Stockhausen', 18 August 2024, https://www.britannica.com/biography/Karlheinz-Stockhausen.

Stockhausen served as sound projectionist for the Cologne performance.[3] And, another year later, he started on his 'first acknowledged masterpiece', *Gesang der Jünglinge* (Song of the Youths).[4]

This piece was a landmark in fusing the concrete sounds of Schaeffer's school with the artificial tones of the Cologne studio. Predating Varèse's *Poème électronique* by a couple of years, Stockhausen's composition was the first major work to bring these opposing styles of electronic music together.

For his artificial sounds, Stockhausen relied heavily on sine tones. These electronically generated noises are among the blandest musical sounds imaginable: flat tones devoid of any characteristic timbre and completely unwavering in pitch and intensity. This may not sound like the most promising material for composition. But by layering multiple sine tones, each with a different pitch and volume, Stockhausen constructed strange musical textures. To these, he added white noise, as well as pulses and clicks created using an impulse generator.

Alongside these artificial sounds, Stockhausen incorporated recordings of a boy singing. But rather than contrasting this organic sound with his electronic tones, Stockhausen sought to weave the two together. He played the sine tones to the child over headphones and asked him to replicate them with

---

[3]Gillian Moore, 'Stockhausen: Portrait of an Electronic Music Pioneer', *The Guardian*, 13 November 2008, https://www.theguardian.com/music/2008/nov/12/squarepusher-karlheinz-stockhausen.
[4]James Nice, *A Young Person's Guide to the Avant-Garde* [CD liner notes], LTM Recordings, 2013.

his singing. Stockhausen also edited the tape, cutting the boy's voice into fragments that complemented the artificial sounds.[5]

These edits drew attention to the boy's words as well, sometimes illuminating their meaning and sometimes obfuscating them with sharp cuts. Despite this fragmentary approach, the lyrics seemed important to Stockhausen. He took them from a Bible story about three young men who are cast into a fiery pit for refusing to worship a false idol. At the end of the story, the youths miraculously emerge from the furnace unharmed. The impressed king declares their god to be true and promotes them to lofty positions in his government.[6]

It's tempting to find parallels between Stockhausen's life and this biblical tale. By merging concrete and artificial sounds, he was refusing to bow to the idolatry of the Paris and Cologne schools. At first, it seemed like he might be tossed into a fiery pit of his own for such radical experimentation. One memorable review declared, '[I]f this is music it's time to drop the H-bomb.'[7] But gradually, *Gesang der Jünglinge* gained a reputation as 'the first true masterwork of electronic music.'[8]

Emerging unscathed from the fires of criticism, Stockhausen even drew praise from the king-like figure he had betrayed: Pierre Schaeffer declared his composition as one of the 'most remarkable so-called electronic works.'[9] In this way, *Gesang*

[5]Thom Holmes, *Electronic and Experimental Music: Technology, Music, and Culture*, sixth edition (New York: Routledge, 2020), 244–6.
[6]The Book of Daniel 3.
[7]Albert Goldberg, 'The Sounding Board: Strange Music Heard at Monday Concert', *Los Angeles Times*, 12 March 1957.
[8]Nice.
[9]Pierre Schaeffer, *Treatise on Musical Objects: An Essay Across Disciples*, trans. Christine North & John Dack (University of California Press, 2017), 9.

der Jünglinge marked a turning point. As one contemporary noted, 'From that point on, we can say that no basic conceptual difference existed between the schools of Paris and Cologne.'[10]

Having shattered these boundaries within electronic music, Stockhausen continued to experiment with other genres and ideas in equally radical ways. His next major work, *Gruppen* (Groups), was composed for three orchestras, each playing at a different tempo from the others.[11] For another piece, *Kontakte* (Contacts), Stockhausen built a rotating platform to capture 'the effect of sounds spinning' through four separate microphones.[12] Between 1962 and 1969, he composed *Momente* (Moments), which employed such eccentric instrumentation as 'tuned cardboard tubes with glued-on lids' and sealed plastic containers filled with 'a small amount of buckshot'.[13]

Although he was a generation older, Stockhausen – and his free-spirited experimentation – were in step with contemporary youth culture. From the Swinging Sixties in London to the hippie movement in San Francisco, the emerging ethos of the decade was founded on artistic liberty – a rebellion against the rules-based order of previous times.

In 1966, when The Mothers of Invention released their landmark album of experimental rock, *Freak Out!*, they

---

[10]Gustav Chiamaga, 'The Tape Studio', in *The Development and Practice of Electronic Music*, ed. Jon H. Appleton & Ronald C. Perera (Englewood Cliffs: Prentice-Hall Inc., 1975), 72.

[11]Karlheinz Stockhausen, *Gruppen/Groups*, http://www.karlheinzstockhausen.org/gruppen_english.htm.

[12]Holmes, 247.

[13]Karlheinz Stockhausen, *Momente/Moments*, http://www.karlheinzstockhausen.org/moment_preface_english.htm.

namechecked Stockhausen on the back cover. That same year, he arrived at the Davis campus of the University of California for a 6-month residency, cementing his influence among the west coast American music scene. 'He became a cultural hero in San Francisco,' one former student recalled, remembering 'jamming sessions with the Grateful Dead.'[14] The band recorded their second album *Anthem of the Sun* around that time – a record that would take them in a more experimental direction. And the influence was clear. 'It had to do with an approach that's more like electronic music or concrète music,' band leader Jerry Garcia said.[15]

But Stockhausen's influence was not limited to California. Returning to his native Germany, he taught Irmin Schmidt and Holger Czukay, who later founded the influential Krautrock band Can. When Stockhausen heard the group's experimental rock music, he reportedly said, 'Well, of course it's good – these were my students.'[16]

Stockhausen generated significant interest in the UK as well. Band members from Pink Floyd and King Crimson acknowledged his influence.[17] The Who even recognized him

[14] Jonathan D. Kramer, 'Karlheinz in California: A Personal Reminiscence', *Perspectives of New Music* 36, no. 1 (Winter, 1998): 247–61.

[15] Simon Reynolds, 'Synthedelia: Psychedelic Electronic Music in the 1960s', *Red Bull Music Academy*, 2 May 2018, https://daily.redbullmusicacademy.com/2018/05/synthedelia.

[16] Alexis Petridis, '"I Grew up in Total Ruins": Irmin Schmidt of Can on LSD, Mourning and Musical Adventures', *The Guardian*, 31 May 2018, https://www.theguardian.com/culture/2018/may/31/i-grew-up-in-total-ruins-irmin-schmidt-of-can-on-lsd-mourning-and-musical-adventures.

[17] Edward Macan, *Rocking the Classics: English Progressive Rock and the Counterculture* (Oxford: Oxford University Press, 1997), 141 & 147–8.

on the back of an album, with a note describing guitarist Pete Townshend's 'interest in Stockhausen, brandy and painting.'[18]

But the German's biggest accolade came in 1967 when he finally appeared on the front of a major rock album – no longer buried in the small print of the liner notes. And it just so happened to be an album by the biggest band in the world: The Beatles.

Granted, Stockhausen was one of the more than fifty figures on the cover of *Sgt. Pepper's Lonely Hearts Club Band*. But each had been carefully selected. 'I asked the four Beatles for a list and I did one myself,' recalled Peter Blake, co-creator of the album design.[19]

It's not certain who requested Stockhausen. But the band were clearly keen to include him. After an initial request for permission went unanswered, the group's manager, Brian Epstein, followed up with an urgent telegram to ensure the composer could appear on the final cover. (For those who have the sleeve to hand, Stockhausen is fifth from the left on the top row, sandwiched between Lenny Bruce and W. C. Fields.)

Stockhausen's image was not just for show. It also signalled an influence on the music inside. 'I was getting interested in *avant garde* things,' Paul McCartney later reflected, calling himself a 'Stockhausen freak.'[20]

One example of this avant-garde approach came on the album's final track 'A Day in the Life', which included an

---

[18] The Who, *Happy Jack* [LP liner notes], Decca Records, USA, 1967.
[19] Spencer Leigh, *Love Me Do to Love Me Don't: The Beatles on Record* (Carmarthen: McNidder & Grace, 2016), 164.
[20] Mark Lewisohn, *The Complete Beatles Recording Sessions* (London: The Hamlyn Publishing Group Limited, 1988), 14.

unconventional orchestral crescendo. McCartney instructed the session musicians to 'go through all the notes on your instrument from the lowest to the highest'. With all the performers playing out of synch, it 'made for a great noise'.[21]

This wasn't the only avant-garde element of the album: hidden at the very end was a piece of pure musique concrète. The band inserted this mysterious micro-track into the run-out groove of the record – a closed loop in which the phonograph needle circles around until it is removed by the listener. Typically, run-out grooves contain no sound; they are just there to prevent the needle from wandering after a record ends. But The Beatles realized this quirk of the vinyl format might provide an interesting way to conclude their album. As audio engineer Geoff Emerick recalled, '[T]he decision to throw in a bit of nonsense gibberish came together in about 10 minutes.'[22] But, perhaps unbeknownst to the band, in creating this 'nonsense gibberish' they were replicating the techniques of musique concrète.

Like all musique concrète compositions, the work began by gathering recorded sound material. As Emerick remembered, '[W]e recorded [the band] twice – one each track of a two-track tape. They made funny noises, said random things; just nonsense.' The next stage was to manipulate the recording. 'We chopped up the tape, put it back together, played it backwards and threw it in,' Emerick said.[23]

[21] Lewisohn, 14.
[22] Lewisohn, 109.
[23] Lewisohn, 109.

The result was a disorienting collage of unrecognizable vocal fragments – similar to the more abrupt edits of the boy's voice in Stockhausen's *Gesang der Jünglinge*. The band may not have been conscious of the parallels to musique concrète at the time. But in their spontaneity, they created a short piece that replicated the conventions of that genre with remarkable precision. Even the fact that they placed their composition within a locked groove harked back to Pierre Schaeffer's earliest experiments.

As it turns out, The Beatles were also in tune with the future direction of musique concrète. Stockhausen's next work, *Hymnen* (Anthems), was a 113-minute epic, based around electronic and concrete reconstructions of various national anthems. As one writer described it, Stockhausen's composition transformed the British national anthem 'into morse code-like bleeps' and manipulated crowd noises into 'ducks that quack the Marseillaise'.[24]

At the same time, The Beatles were working on a world anthem of their own. Their song 'All You Need is Love' was being developed for a special programme, to be broadcast via 'the world's first television satellite link-up'.[25] Although they could not have heard Stockhausen's work in progress (it would premiere a few months after their TV broadcast), The Beatles paralleled some of his ideas. They too included a section from the French anthem 'La Marseillaise' within their song. They also interpolated extracts from several other pieces of

[24] Robert Worby, 'Crackle goes pop: how Stockhausen seduced the Beatles', *The Guardian*, 26 December 2015, https://www.theguardian.com/music/2015/dec/26/beatles-revolution-9-stockhausen-hymnen-avant-garde-pop.
[25] Lewisohn, 116.

world music in their instrumentation. 'We played bits of Bach's Brandenburg concerto,' one session musician recalled. There were also references to the English folk tune 'Greensleeves', the American big band jazz standard 'In the Mood', and even The Beatles' own song 'She Loves You'.[26]

Of course, 'All You Need is Love' was still very much in the pop idiom. It was a far cry from the dense experimentation of Stockhausen, which would strike most ears as unlistenable. But the individual band members seemed interested in exploring a more challenging avant-garde direction, as exemplified by their solo projects of the same period.

Paul McCartney may have been the first Beatle to venture into the deep end of the avant-garde. In 1967, he was commissioned to produce a tape for the Million Volt Light and Sound Rave. This art festival, held at London's Roundhouse, would be a showcase for new sounds in electronic music. Delia Derbyshire, that pioneering experimenter from the BBC's Radiophonic Workshop, was among those on the bill.[27]

For his contribution, McCartney recruited his bandmates during a studio session, asking them to 'wander round all of the stuff and bang it, shout, play it'.[28] The resulting chaos included 'distorted, hypnotic drum and organ sounds' as well as McCartney and John Lennon yelling random phrases, such as 'Are you all right?' and 'Barcelona!'.[29]

---

[26] Lewisohn, 120.
[27] Holmes, 353.
[28] Vanessa Thorpe, 'Forty Years On, McCartney Wants the World to Hear "Lost" Beatles Epic', *The Guardian*, 16 November 2008, https://www.theguardian.com/music/2008/nov/16/paul-mccartney-carnival-of-light.
[29] Lewisohn, 92.

The tape was assembled with various overdubs and echo effects, clocking in at 13 minutes – the same length as Stockhausen's *Gesang der Jünglinge*. But the finished piece, titled 'Carnival of Light', was not constructed with the same care. Whereas Stockhausen took 2 years to realize his piece, 'Carnival of Light' was 'knocked off quickly'.[30]

This haphazard approach may explain why the piece was quietly sealed away in the vaults after its premiere. It was never released again during the band's lifetime. In the 1990s, it was vetoed from inclusion in their retrospective *Anthology* series.[31] And in 2025, when another *Anthology* album was released, the track was excluded yet again![32]

Some of the band's members were not only sceptical of this track – they questioned the whole concept of the avant-garde. Lennon supposedly quipped that the phrase was 'French for bullshit'. George Harrison reportedly translated it as 'Haven't garde a clue'.[33]

Despite this, they soon began solo experiments of their own. Harrison was first, producing a soundtrack for the 1968 film *Wonderwall*. The album was largely a vehicle for his interest in Indian music. But some tracks incorporated concrete elements as well. For instance, he assembled 'Dream Scene' by stitching recordings together from several different

[30] Ian MacDonald, *Revolution in the Head: The Beatles' Records and the Sixties*, third revised edition (London: Vintage Books, 2008), 225.
[31] Ian Winwood, 'Carnival of Light: The Demented History of the "Lost" Beatles Song You'll Never Hear', *The Telegraph*, 2 November 2023, https://www.telegraph.co.uk/music/artists/now-and-then-the-beatles-carnival-of-light-lost-song/.
[32] The Beatles, *Anthology 4* [CD], Apple Records, UK, 2025.
[33] Winwood.

sessions, adding tape loops and backwards sound effects.[34] It also included elements of sound collage, drawing on samples from the Abbey Road library.[35]

But the Beatle who delved furthest into musique concrète was Lennon. While McCartney claimed he was first to dabble in the avant-garde through his connections to the 'London crowd',[36] Lennon made the opposite argument. By 'hiding in Weybridge', a suburb west of London, Lennon suggested that he was able to find the peace and isolation needed for true creativity. 'We used to be a bit supercritical of each other,' Lennon said of his bandmates. '[W]e inhibited each other.'[37] In his country retreat, Lennon was free to make 'hours of tape of different sounds' without fear of embarrassment. 'I suppose you would call them avant-garde,' he reflected. But his experiments remained private. 'There were very few people I could play those tapes to,' he said.[38]

Eventually, Lennon found someone he felt comfortable sharing them with: performance artist Yoko Ono. The two met at London's Indica Gallery, where Ono was putting on an exhibition. After several more meetings and a period of correspondence, Lennon invited her to his home on 19 May 1968.[39] '[W]e went upstairs to my studio and I played her all the

[34] Richard S. Ginell, '*Wonderwall Music* review', *AllMusic*, https://www.allmusic.com/album/wonderwall-music-mw0000676515.
[35] Matt Hurwitz, 'Wonderwall Music', *GeorgeHarrison.com*, 18 February 2020, https://www.georgeharrison.com/features/wonderwall-music/.
[36] Lewisohn, 14.
[37] Jann Wenner, 'The Rolling Stone Interview: John Lennon, Part One: The Working Class Hero', *Rolling Stone*, 21 January 1971, https://www.johnlennon.com/music/interviews/rolling-stone-interview-1970/.
[38] Wenner, 'The Rolling Stone Interview: John Lennon, Part One.'
[39] MacDonald, 281.

tapes that I'd made, all this far-out stuff, some comedy stuff, and some electronic music. She was suitably impressed.'[40] Ono then suggested they make some tapes of their own. Starting at midnight, the pair assembled a strange collage consisting of snippets of their conversation, Ono's wailing, and Lennon's tape loops. According to Lennon, the couple completed the composition by dawn, at which point they consummated their relationship. 'It was very beautiful,' he said.[41]

The work was released as an album called *Unfinished Music No. 1: Two Virgins*. Despite bearing the name of a Beatle, it failed to chart in the United Kingdom. In the United States, it entered the charts at No. 158,[42] eventually peaking at 124.[43] Its lacklustre performance suggested that the public weren't ready for something so radical – an album from a Beatle without lyrics, melody or even a beat.

But sales of *Two Virgins* may also have been harmed by its cover image: a full-length nude photograph of the couple. In the United States, the record label declined 'reviewer, promotion and disk jockey copies to avoid creating a nude-teaser campaign.'[44] A few weeks later, two men were arrested in Chicago on obscenity charges for displaying the album art in a store window.[45] In New Jersey, police confiscated 30,000

[40] Jann Wenner, 'The Rolling Stone Interview: John Lennon, Part Two: Life With the Lions', *Rolling Stone*, 4 February 1971, https://www.johnlennon.com/music/interviews/rolling-stone-interview-1970/.
[41] Wenner, 'The Rolling Stone Interview: John Lennon, Part Two.'
[42] *Billboard*, 8 February 1969, 80.
[43] *Billboard*, 22 March 1969, 76.
[44] *Billboard*, 16 November 1968, 84.
[45] *Billboard*, 21 December 1968, 46.

copies of the record being unloaded from a plane.[46] Across the border, a Canadian politician brandished a copy in the House of Commons, decrying it as 'foreign-made pornographic material'.[47]

But Lennon and Ono's intentions were more innocent. They took out a full-page advertisement in *Billboard* magazine to reflect this. It consisted simply of a Bible verse describing the prelapsarian Adam and Eve: 'And they were both naked, the man and his wife, and were not ashamed'.[48] The album's contents reflected this innocence, showcasing an uninhibited willingness to experiment within the playground of the avant-garde – to approach music as children again, freely and without regard for mainstream conventions.

Despite being a commercial failure by Lennon's standards, *Two Virgins* nonetheless brought musique concrète to wider audiences. Before it had even broken into the charts, the album had sold over 150,000 copies 'primarily under-the-counter' in the United States.[49] Distribution deals were also struck in France, Holland and Israel, giving it an international reach.[50] This was the kind of exposure composers like Stockhausen would rarely achieve. So, even if it wasn't 'pure' musique concrète, it nonetheless became one of the most widely heard artefacts of that genre as soon as it was released.

---

[46] *Billboard*, 18 January 1969, 100.
[47] *Billboard*, 29 March 1969, 60.
[48] *Billboard*, 11 January 1969, 21.
[49] *Billboard*, 1 February 1969, 3.
[50] *Billboard*, 11 January 1969, 48.

As for the question of influence, Lennon attributed everything to Ono. 'I'm influenced by her music 1,000 per cent more than I ever was by anybody or anything,' he said.[51]

But Ono herself was well-schooled in the avant-garde. Although her early work focused on written, visual and performance art, she moved in musical circles. Her first husband, Toshi Ichiyanagi, was an avant-garde composer who had worked at a Japanese studio modelled on the Cologne approach.[52] She knew proto-concrete pioneer John Cage and was certainly familiar with composers like Varèse and Stockhausen.[53] When a retrospective box set of her music was released in 1992, the liner notes stated that *Two Virgins* 'was explicitly inspired by the work Karlheinz Stockhausen and other "classical" composers were doing at the time.'[54]

The couple seemed to acknowledge their debt to the German composer when they sent him a Christmas card in 1969.[55] And since then, Lennon and Stockhausen have continued to be linked in the cultural imagination. A rumour that the pair once considered a joint concert was the basis of a 2011 theatre show. The scriptwriter, Andrew Kupfer, argued that the two are united not only by their genre-pushing tendencies, but also by a utopian outlook that made them

[51] Wenner, 'The Rolling Stone Interview: John Lennon, Part One.'

[52] Emmanuelle Loubet, Curtis Roads & Brigitte Robindoré, 'The Beginnings of Electronic Music in Japan, with a Focus on the NHK Studio: The 1950s and 1960s', *Computer Music Journal* 21, no. 4 (1997): 11–22.

[53] Yoko Ono, 'My memory of Stefan Wolpe', *Imagine Peace*, 2002, https://www.imaginepeace.com/archives/8682.

[54] Robert Palmer, 'On Thin Ice – The Music of Yoko Ono', *Onobox*, 1992.

[55] Alex Ross, 'The Beatles and the Avant-Garde', *The New Yorker*, 23 February 2010, https://www.newyorker.com/culture/alex-ross/the-beatles-and-the-avant-garde.

quasi-religious figures. '[T]hey believed that the forces of the establishment would be swept away and new, wonderful things would come in their place,' Kupfer said.[56]

Indeed, by 1968 Stockhausen was already being 'acclaimed as a musical Messiah'.[57] He continued to be seen as a kind of prophet by subsequent generations. According to Icelandic singer Björk, 'When Karlheinz harnessed electricity into sound and showed the rest of us, he sparked off a sun that is still burning and will glow for a long time.'[58]

Upon his death in 2007, Stockhausen's messianic qualities were emphasized in a statement from his two 'companions'. They praised him as a man 'who lived to bring celestial music to humans,' before concluding that 'he ascended with joy through heaven's door in order to continue to compose in paradise with cosmic pulses in eternal harmony.'[59]

But for all his messianic qualities, Stockhausen lacked the reach to truly bring the gospel of the avant-garde to the masses. On the other hand, as Lennon infamously declared, The Beatles were 'more popular than Jesus'.[60] So, if anyone was

[56] Allan Kozinn, 'A '60s Mash-Up That Didn't Happen', *The New York Times*, 4 March 2011, https://www.nytimes.com/2011/03/06/arts/music/06alarm.html.
[57] Peter Heyworth, 'The Stockhausen sledgehammer', *The Observer Review*, 7 January 1968.
[58] Björk, 'Why I love Stockhausen', *The Guardian*, 30 October 2008, https://www.theguardian.com/music/2008/oct/30/bjork-karlheinz-stockhausen-electronica.
[59] David Ward, 'Stockhausen, Prolific Music Modernist, Dies Aged 79', *The Guardian*, 8 December 2007, https://www.theguardian.com/world/2007/dec/08/filmandmusic1.germany.
[60] Maureen Cleave, 'How Does a Beatle Live? John Lennon Lives Like This', *The Evening Standard*, 4 March 1966.

going to spread musique concrète further across the world, it would be them.

A concrete pairing: Karlheinz Stockhausen and The Beatles

In the same interview that Paul McCartney declared himself a 'Stockhausen freak', he also made a contradictory statement. 'There was only one Stockhausen song I liked,' McCartney claimed. 'I thought most of his other stuff was too fruity.'[61]

The piece favoured by McCartney was *Gesang der Jünglinge* (Song of the Youths) – the 1956 composition in which Karlheinz Stockhausen blended French concrete techniques with German artificial tones.

In Beatles lore, this work is closely associated with their 1966 song 'Tomorrow Never Knows'. The track is notable for its use of loops – segments of tape spliced end to end, creating repeating patterns or layered sounds. While Stockhausen had been experimenting with loops since his earliest days at the Paris studio in 1952, they were a relatively new concept to The Beatles.

'The tape loop idea started because they all had Brennell [*sic*] machines,' audio engineer Geoff Emerick recalled.[62] These were small recorders which could be used at home to edit tape and apply various effects. John Lennon used them to create

[61] Lewisohn, 15.
[62] Lewisohn, 72.

his album *Unfinished Music No. 1: Two Virgins* with Yoko Ono.[63] He later claimed to own as many as ten of the machines.[64]

'Paul in particular used to make his own loops at home and walk into the studio with bags full of little reels,' Emerick continued. For 'Tomorrow Never Knows' McCartney's tape loops largely drew on recordings of musical sounds. These included 'an orchestral chord', a sitar scale, and notes from a Mellotron (an electro-mechanical precursor to the synthesiser).[65]

McCartney manipulated these recordings to create his finished loops through a process known as tape saturation. This involves 'recording over and over on the same piece of tape.'[66] He also experimented with accelerating the tapes[67] and with slowing them down. 'One of the things we discovered when playing around with loops on 'Tomorrow Never Knows' was that the texture and depth of certain instruments sounded really good when slowed down,' Emerick recalled.[68]

The band recorded the foundation of the song live in the studio, using drums, guitars, bass and more.[69] They added McCartney's loops the following day. 'All over the studio we had people spooling them onto machines with pencils,' producer George Martin recalled. As audio engineer Phil

[63] Paul McCartney, Rock & Roll Hall of Fame induction speech for John Lennon, 1994, https://rockhall.com/inductees/john-lennon/.
[64] Wenner, 'The Rolling Stone Interview: John Lennon, Part Two.'
[65] MacDonald, 190–1.
[66] Lewisohn, 72.
[67] MacDonald, 190.
[68] Lewisohn, 74.
[69] Lewisohn, 70.

McDonald remembered, the 'control room was as full of loops as it was people.'[70]

On the finished track, five different loops are easily distinguishable to the ear.[71] The most prominent is a 'seagull' effect. So notable was this sound that it was lampooned a few months after the song's release as part of a BBC comedy special. In the sketch, comedians Peter Cook and Dudley Moore perform a psychedelic parody song, titled 'The L. S. Bumble Bee'. Towards the end of the piece, a seagull sound effect intrudes, only for the camera to pan across to reveal an actual seagull. (Incidentally, John Lennon made a cameo in another sketch on the programme, playing a lavatory attendant. His participation suggests there were no hard feelings for this gentle ribbing.)[72]

Despite the seagull being one of their most recognizable sound effects, how The Beatles created it remains a subject of disagreement. It has been variously identified as 'a distorted guitar'[73] or a manipulated recording of McCartney laughing.[74] The fact that the sound source cannot be conclusively identified bolsters the song's concrete credentials. Indeed, as one musicologist defined it, musique concrète must be

---

[70] Lewisohn, 72.

[71] MacDonald, 190.

[72] Andrew Martin, 'Sunday Post: Not Only . . . But Also - The Missing Minutes', *BBC Genome Blog*, 21 February 2016, https://www.bbc.co.uk/webarchive/https%3A%2F%2Fwww.bbc.co.uk%2Fblogs%2Fgenome%2Fentries%2F56b0ca36-b440-4dcb-91e2-d220123ad5e8.

[73] Lewisohn, 72.

[74] MacDonald, 190.

composed of sounds 'whose origin it is not always possible to distinguish'.[75]

Of course, the band's inspiration, Stockhausen, did not restrict himself to such rigid doctrines. But perhaps he would have been proud of The Beatles for their avant-pop innovation anyway – even if they did find his music 'too fruity'.

For your recommended listening experience, please pair:

'Gesang der Jünglinge' by Karlheinz Stockhausen, 1956 (13:05)
with
'Tomorrow Never Knows' by The Beatles, 1966 (2:58)

[75] Holmes, 213.

8 The Beatles and Revolution 9

As the 1960s counterculture reached its apex, musique concrète became inescapable. Even on an album of steel-string guitar instrumentals, you might be confronted with its weirdness.

Such was the work of John Fahey, an American fingerstyle player judged to be one of the greatest of all time.[1] He was barely out of his teens when he started self-releasing albums of his solo guitar music. Then, in 1967, he was offered a record contract. Fahey should have been right at home among the label's roster of folk artists, but he broke away, filling his commercial debut with an extended exercise in musique concrète. Bizarrely, he had never even listened to an example of the genre before.[2]

'Somewhere along the line I heard the word "collage" and it stuck with me,' he reflected years later. Fahey's concrete experiment started with a base layer of guitar noodling. Over this he added farm animal noises, fairground sounds, fragments from old blues records, and snippets from the speeches of Adolf Hitler. 'I wanted to do it,' was his simple justification. '[I]t was a statement I had to make.'[3]

---

[1] 'The 250 Greatest Guitarists of All Time', *Rolling Stone*, 13 October 2023, https://www.rollingstone.com/music/music-lists/best-guitarists-1234814010/.
[2] Edwin Pouncey, 'Blood on the Frets', *The Wire* #174, August 1998.
[3] Pouncey.

What exactly Fahey's statement was may not be clear. But other artists of the time clearly felt a similar urge. For example, The Doors flirted with psychedelic weirdness on their self-titled debut album – and decided to take things further for the follow-up, 1967's *Strange Days*. In keeping with the times, this included throwing in a 'musique concrète track of wild shit,' as drummer John Densmore described it.[4]

The track, titled 'Horse Latitudes,' was built around a white noise recording manipulated to sound like the wind. Over this, the band 'played musical instruments in unusual ways,' with the sounds altered electronically. They also 'dropped a Coke bottle into a metal trashcan, beat coconut shells on a tile floor, and had some friends wail their lungs raw.'[5]

As Densmore recalled, fellow California rockers Jefferson Airplane visited the studio on the day 'Horse Latitudes' was recorded. 'They thought that we had left the planet and gone to Mars,' he remembered. But the Airplane must have changed their minds, because their next album featured a musique concrète–inspired track of its own, titled 'A Small Package of Value Will Come to You, Shortly.'[6]

Other major artists of the time were also experimenting with sound collage. David Bowie ended his 1967 debut album with a curious song titled 'Please Mr. Gravedigger.' The track features no instruments, only Bowie singing over a series of

[4] Samuel Andreyev, 'The Doors Drummer John Densmore: Music and Culture in the 1960s,' [Video interview], 26 July 2024, https://www.youtube.com/watch?v=REQPSK-8m14&ab_channel=SamuelAndreyev.
[5] Jerry Hopkins & Danny Sugerman, *No One Here Gets Out Alive* (New York: Plexus Publishing Ltd: 1980), 127–8.
[6] Andreyev.

sound effects. The Lovin' Spoonful went further with the 7-minute track 'War Games', which begins with the noises of a woman giving birth and then tells the story of her son's life entirely through recorded sounds. These include a recitation of the Pledge of Allegiance, an extract from an army recruitment commercial, and (perhaps inevitably for the Vietnam War era) a massive explosion to signal the character's end.

Folk duo Simon and Garfunkel also used sound collage. In 1966, they layered a fabricated news bulletin over the Christmas song 'Silent Night', drawing a contrast between society's ills and the cheeriness of the festive period. In 1968, they released a track of pure sound collage called 'Voices of Old People'. As its title suggests, the piece consists entirely of recordings gathered from nursing homes.[7]

As these examples illustrate, recorded sounds of all kinds were increasingly becoming part of the vocabulary of popular music in the mid- to late-1960s. And it was in this context that The Beatles entered the studio to record their next opus, known colloquially as *The White Album*. This record would be their longest and most eclectic work yet, drawing on genres as diverse as reggae, country, music hall, baroque pop, and even lullabies. Into this mix also came musique concrète. While the band had been inspired by that genre before, they had never released a work entirely in its idiom. But now, with the album's penultimate track, 'Revolution 9', they would finally abandon any pretence of pop and fully immerse themselves in this avant-garde genre.

[7]Spencer Leigh, *Simon & Garfunkel: Together Alone* (Carmarthen: McNidder & Grace: 2016), 75.

But what made 'Revolution 9' so significant? After all – as the examples above illustrate – many popular artists were experimenting with sound collage and musique concrète prior to the Fab Four.

Well, firstly, The Beatles created a piece that was much more substantial than some of those earlier efforts. The tracks by The Doors and Jefferson Airplane both came in at well under 2 minutes; 'Revolution 9' lasted over eight.

'Revolution 9' was also more substantial from the point of view of complexity and structure. For example, while The Lovin' Spoonful created a sound collage that was almost equally lengthy, it conveyed a rather obvious narrative by simply stitching together one-dimensional sound samples. In contrast, 'Revolution 9' was sinister and mysterious, layering disguised and manipulated sounds on top of each other to confound any singular interpretation. Yet it still retained an underlying structure – discernible to the discriminating listener.

Finally, 'Revolution 9' was significant simply because The Beatles were bigger than anyone else. *The White Album* spent 8 weeks at No. 1 in the United States[8] and 9 weeks in the top position in the United Kingdom.[9] Within days of its release, copies were in around a million homes. So, purely by virtue of being included on the album, 'Revolution 9' immediately

[8]'Chart History: The Beatles', *Billboard*, https://www.billboard.com/artist/the-beatles/chart-history/tlp/.
[9]'Official Charts: The Beatles', *Official Charts*, https://www.officialcharts.com/artist/10363/beatles/.

became 'the world's most widely distributed avant-garde artefact'.[10]

The track began to emerge on 30 May 1968 – the first day of recording for the new album. The Beatles had entered the studio to work on a relatively simple blues shuffle song, supported by piano, acoustic guitar and drums.[11] Its working title, 'Revolution', suggested something radical. But the lyrics confounded the expectations of the cultural moment, arguing against violent rebellion with the reassurance that everything was 'gonna be all right'.

The band recorded the song more than a dozen times that day, with each take 'averaging about five minutes'. But something changed with take eighteen. The group continued playing past their usual point, transitioning into an extended jam that brought the track length to over 10 minutes. This improvised outro descended into chaos, incorporating feedback, clattering piano and increasingly erratic vocals from John Lennon, whose repetitions of 'all right' devolved from singing to shouting to screeching.[12]

With the song earmarked as a possible single, there was no way it could be released in its 10-minute form. So, the band broke the track in two. The first half formed the basis for the more conventional blues-rock song. Meanwhile, the second

[10] Ian MacDonald, *Revolution in the Head: The Beatles' Records and the Sixties*, third revised edition (London: Vintage Books, 2008), 287.
[11] Mark Lewisohn, *The Complete Beatles Recording Sessions* (London: The Hamlyn Publishing Group Limited, 1988), 135.
[12] Lewisohn, 135.

half was reserved as a template for the avant-garde experiment which would become 'Revolution 9'.[13]

The album sessions came less than 2 weeks after Lennon and his new girlfriend Yoko Ono had recorded *Unfinished Music No. 1: Two Virgins* – their 'musique concrète first kiss'.[14] So, it was no surprise that Lennon spearheaded this next audacious offshoot into the avant-garde. Indeed, although the track is credited to The Beatles, much of the work was done by Lennon alone. 'John was really the producer of "Revolution 9"', clarified Richard Lush, who served as an engineer on *The White Album*.[15]

The work began by digging up sound samples from the library at EMI Recording Studios. 'There were many loops and tapes,' Lennon recalled. 'I was cutting up Beethoven and playing him backwards, anything I could lay me hands on.'[16] He synchronized these tape fragments over the chaotic outro from take eighteen of 'Revolution'. But as the musique concrète composition progressed, Lennon largely removed the backing track. This left the sound samples to stand alone, merely implying the rhythm and structure of the original in an abstract manner.

Although Lennon led the project, George Harrison also contributed to 'Revolution 9'. In one session, he and Lennon read out a series of random statements to be added to the track – recalling a similar technique from the 'Carnival of Light' recording the previous year. This time, the phrases included

---

[13] Lewisohn, 135.

[14] John Lennon & Yoko Ono, *Unfinished Music No. 1: Two Virgins* [CD reissue promotional sticker], Secretly Canadian, 2016.

[15] Lewisohn, 138.

[16] Jerry Levitan, *I Met the Walrus* (New York: HarperCollins Publishers, 2009), 99.

'financial imbalance', 'Eldorado', and 'take this brother, may it serve you well'.[17]

But Harrison also claimed a more substantial contribution. As he remembered, it was him and drummer Ringo Starr who collected the sound samples for the track. 'We went into the tape library and looked through the entire room and pulled main selections and then gave the tapes to John and he cut them together,' Harrison said. 'John sat there and decided what bits to cross-fade together, but if Ringo and I hadn't gone up there in the first place he wouldn't have had anything.'[18]

Ono was another key collaborator. Like Harrison, she made some vocal contributions, including the memorable closing line, 'you become naked'. But Ono also acted as a kind of avant-garde muse. 'John brought her into the control room of number three at the start of the "White Album" sessions,' engineer Geoff Emerick remembered. 'She was always by his side after that.'[19] Indeed, as 'Revolution 9' was being completed, Emerick was usurped from his usual spot at the console. Instead, Lennon worked the controls, with Ono next to him.[20] 'Yoko was there for the whole thing and she made decisions about which loops to use,' Lennon later clarified.[21]

Seated at the console, Lennon faded the loops in and out over a playback of the 'Revolution' outro to create a live mix

---

[17] Lewisohn, 138.

[18] Bill Flanagan, 'George Harrison: The Dark Horse Candidate', *Musician* [magazine], September 1992, 43.

[19] Lewisohn, 135.

[20] Lewisohn, 138.

[21] David Sheff, *All We Are Saying: The Last Major Interview with John Lennon and Yoko Ono* (New York: St Martin's Griffin, 2000), 188.

of his track.[22] So abundant were the loops that the session spilled across three studios. Like the recording of 'Tomorrow Never Knows', there were 'people all over EMI Studios spooling loops onto tape machines with pencils'.[23] The sounds from these endless reels encompassed a vast array. They included laughter, crowd chatter, applause, crackling fire, explosions, and numerous extracts from classical music – often chopped into small fragments or played backwards.

Some of these sounds remained identifiable on the finished track. Others were given the concrete treatment of manipulation or overlayering to disguise their origins. But the most important technique for 'Revolution 9' was decontextualization. Rather than physically manipulating sounds, Lennon often just divorced them from their original contexts, changing the way listeners would interpret them.

A key example is Lennon's repeated shout of 'all right' from the 'Revolution' outro. While most of this rhythm track was removed from 'Revolution 9', Lennon kept moments of his vocal refrain intact. But without the rest of the song, Lennon's screams have been variously misinterpreted as 'ride' or 'rise' – overturning the track's original statement that everything was 'gonna be all right'.[24]

The most famous sample was also subject to decontextualization. It consists of a male voice intoning the

[22] 'John Lennon on the Dennis Elsas Show, WNEW-FM, 28 Sept 1974', https://www.johnlennon.com/news/john-lennon-on-the-dennis-elsas-show-wnew-fm-28-september-1974/.
[23] Lewisohn, 138.
[24] Morgan Enos, 'In Defense of "Revolution 9" at 50: Why the Beatles' Most Daring Track Is Still Underrated', *Billboard*, 22 November 2018, https://www.billboard.com/music/rock/the-beatles-revolution-9-white-album-defense-8486236/.

phrase 'number nine'. Different sources credit it as an extract from 'an examination tape'[25] or 'an engineer's testing tape'.[26] But whatever its origins, by excising the 'number nine' from this context, Lennon transformed something banal into something sinister. Its flat, unemotional tones, repeated incessantly across a chaotic soundscape, become less like a boring announcement of an exam question, and more like the dystopian proclamation of a violent uprising.

Indeed, in its simplest terms, 'Revolution 9' might be interpreted as a portrait of violent revolution in sound. Lennon himself described the track as 'an action painting'[27] and 'just like a drawing of revolution'.[28] So, in this way, it acts as a response to the anti-violence blues-rock number that originated it. By cutting up fragments of the cultural cornerstones of classical music, the track sonically describes a breakdown of the normal structures of society. And, through its myriad samples, it portrays the eternal truth of how all revolutions come – with chanting and applause prefiguring the sound of guns and bombs.

Lennon was pleased with the finished result. When later asked what his favourite Beatles songs were, it was the first he mentioned: 'I like my own, you know. I like Revolution 9.'[29]

---

[25] Lewisohn, 138.

[26] Jann Wenner, 'The Rolling Stone Interview: John Lennon, Part Two: Life With the Lions', *Rolling Stone*, 21 January 1971, https://www.johnlennon.com/music/interviews/rolling-stone-interview-1970/.

[27] 'John Lennon on the Dennis Elsas Show.'

[28] Wenner, 'The Rolling Stone Interview: John Lennon, Part Two.'

[29] Ben Beaumont-Thomas, '"I was a Hypocrite on the Make": unheard John Lennon Interviews up for Auction', *The Guardian*, 8 September 2021, https://www.theguardian.com/music/2021/sep/08/john-lennon-interviews-auction-tapes-beatles-yoko-ono.

He even suggested issuing it as a single – with the blues-rock version on the A-side and the musique concrète on the reverse. On this idea, however, he was overruled by the rest of the band. 'It was just, literally, the others wouldn't let me,' Lennon remembered.[30]

Indeed, the other Beatles seemed less enamoured with the work. Engineer Geoff Emerick recalled Harrison and Starr looking 'distinctly embarrassed' when listening to the playback.[31] Paul McCartney was equally unimpressed. 'I can't recall exactly what happened later but I know it *didn't* get a fantastic reaction from McCartney,' engineer Richard Lush said.[32] According to Emerick, McCartney tried to persuade Lennon to leave 'Revolution 9' off *The White Album* entirely. 'I heard through the grapevine that John and Paul ultimately had a huge row,' Emerick recalled. 'Paul absolutely did not want it on the album, and John was just as adamant that it would be on there.'[33] In the end, Lennon won. And so, it was sequenced as the penultimate track and released on an unsuspecting public on 22 November 1968.[34]

The immediate reaction to 'Revolution 9' was just as polarising as the opinions within the band. A reviewer in *Melody Maker* condemned it as 'downright buffoonery'.[35] *The*

[30] Jeff Burger, ed., *Lennon on Lennon: Conversations with John Lennon* (London: Omnibus Press, 2017), 149.
[31] Geoff Emerick & Howard Massey, *Here, There and Everywhere: My Life Recording the Music of The Beatles* (New York: Gotham Books, 2007), 243.
[32] Lewisohn, 138.
[33] Emerick & Massey, 244.
[34] Lewisohn, 163.
[35] Michael Smith, 'Best Songwriters since Schubert? If only Socrates Played Guitar . . . ,' *Melody Maker*, 30 November 1968, 5.

Times judged it to be 'interesting, narcotic, but rather too long'.[36] On a more positive note, *The Guardian* singled out Lennon as 'the most impressive man' in the band, with specific reference to 'Revolution 9'.[37] Likewise, *Rolling Stone* praised the track as 'beautifully organized' and argued that of the two versions of 'Revolution' on the album, it was the musique concrète that had 'the most impact'.[38]

The track continued to draw some praise retrospectively. Fifty years after its release, Allan Kozinn offered a spirited defence of the piece during a Beatles conference at Monmouth University. 'As part of my work as a classical music critic, I run into electronic music and sound collages,' he began. 'But "Revolution 9" seems to me, really, almost in a class by itself. It does the same things that those kinds of pieces do. But it also has, I think, more of a clear narrative edge.'[39]

Despite this, the track has become a mainstay on lists of the worst Beatles recordings. In one of the earliest of such polls, conducted by *Village Voice* in 1971, fans named 'Revolution 9' their least favourite Beatles song of all.[40] Years later, a critic for *The Independent* judged it second worst of the thirty songs on *The White Album*, with only the 50-second throwaway

[36] William Mann, 'The new Beatles Album', *The Times*, 22 November 1968, 9.
[37] Geoffrey Cannon, 'Back to Spring', *The Guardian*, 26 November 1968, https://www.theguardian.com/music/from-the-archive-blog/2018/nov/09/beatles-white-album-review-november-1968.
[38] Jann Wenner, 'Beatles', *Rolling Stone*, 21 December 1968, 10.
[39] Jason Kruppa, '009 It's Gonna Be Alright: Revolution - Part I (Revolution 1 & 9)', *Producing The Beatles: The Podcast*, 22 July 2019, https://www.producingthebeatles.com/new-episodes/2019/7/21/009-its-gonna-be-alright-part-i.
[40] Nicholas Schaffner, *The Beatles Forever* (New York: McGraw-Hill, 1978), 217.

track 'Wild Honey Pie' rated lower.[41] On a comprehensive ranking of 188 Beatles songs, *NME* positioned 'Revolution 9' at number 184. Yet, even with this low placement, the write-up acknowledged the piece as 'more notable and influential than it's often given credit for'.[42]

Lennon himself certainly believed in this influence. The year after 'Revolution 9' was released, he doubled down on his avant-garde direction, producing two more experimental albums with Yoko Ono. '[I]t's going to be pop music in five years what we're doing now,' he declared of these projects.[43]

Of course, it didn't work out that way. The first of these albums, *Unfinished Music No. 2: Life with the Lions*, failed to chart in the UK and peaked at No. 174 in the United States[44] – fifty places lower than *Two Virgins* had managed. The next record, titled *Wedding Album*, limped only as far as No. 178.[45]

But if Lennon retreated from the avant-garde after this, it wasn't simply because of lacklustre sales. It also reflected his natural tendency to never sit still – to constantly try new artistic directions. Even within the trilogy of avant-garde albums, his approach was never the same twice. While *Two Virgins* clung somewhat faithfully to musique concrète, its

41 Jacob Stolworthy, 'The Beatles' White Album Tracks, Ranked – From Blackbird to While My Guitar Gently Weeps', *The Independent*, 30 May 2022, https://www.independent.co.uk/arts-entertainment/music/features/the-beatles-white-album-tracks-ranked-paul-mccartney-john-lennon-george-harrison-50-anniversary-b2090627.html.

42 Mark Beaumont, 'The Beatles: Every Song Ranked in Order of Greatness', *NME*, 2 November 2023, https://www.nme.com/features/the-beatles-every-song-ranked-3121214.

43 Levitan, 95.

44 *Billboard*, 2 August 1969, 69.

45 *Billboard*, 27 December 1969, 47.

follow-ups explored other territories. For instance, *Life with the Lions* centred around a 26-minute live recording of Lennon's electric guitar feedback and Ono's screeching. On *Wedding Album*, the classic musique concrète sound of heartbeats was used. But it remained in the background, serving as a sound bed for 22-minutes of Lennon and Ono calling each other's names in increasingly orgasmic fashion.

This constant shifting of style and approach was part of what defined Lennon and The Beatles. They stood in contrast to the originators of musique concrète and electronic music – those products of the age of manifesto, carefully defining rules for composition in their studios in Paris and Cologne.

As Paul McCartney reflected years later, 'what made the Beatles such a great band was that no two tracks are the same'.[46] There was no singular template or rulebook they followed. And so, it is perfectly fitting that they should have created the most widely distributed work of musique concrète ever heard, only to immediately abandon the genre and never return to it again.

A concrete pairing: The Beatles and The Avalanches

In 1968, The Beatles filled *The White Album* with sound effects. The record opens with the noise of a plane taking off for 'Back

[46]Paul Muldoon, 'Ken Dodd, Stockhausen and Psycho: Unlocking Paul McCartney's Musical Genius', *The Guardian*, 30 October 2021, https://www.theguardian.com/music/2021/oct/30/his-lyrics-defined-the-times-paul-muldoon-on-working-with-paul-mccartney.

in the U.S.S.R'. The snorting of swine adds texture to the song 'Piggies'. And, for 'Blackbird', the twittering of the titular bird underpins an otherwise sparse guitar and vocal arrangement.

But 'Revolution 9' was different. It didn't just include recorded sound samples as an add-on – it was composed almost entirely out of them. As music critic Robert Christgau declared, it was a Beatles track on which 'there were no Beatles'.[47]

The band could produce a piece like this because of their singular commercial clout. It gave them free rein to plunder the EMI sound library, and limitless studio time to experiment with the audio they found there. Few other artists of the period had such luxuries.

But, in subsequent decades, recorded sound became more easily obtainable. The evolution from phonograph, to tape, to compact disc, to digital download, made audio increasingly accessible – and simpler to edit without pricey studio equipment.

Gradually, this enabled sampling to become part of the musical landscape. Though the technique is most associated with hip-hop, it also gave rise to a type of music known as plunderphonics. Similarly to 'Revolution 9', this genre puts sampled material front and centre by creating tracks entirely from previously recorded sounds.

One of the seminal artists of plunderphonics is electronic music group The Avalanches. Their 2000 debut album, *Since I Left You*, includes more than 900 distinct samples.[48] For the

[47] Robert Christgau, *Grown Up All Wrong: 75 Great Rock and Pop Artists from Vaudeville to Techno* (Cambridge, MA: Harvard University Press, 1998), 119.
[48] Matt LeMay, 'Since I Left You, The Avalanches', *Pitchfork*, https://pitchfork.com/reviews/albums/385-since-i-left-you/.

breakout single, 'Frontier Psychiatrist', these include jazz guitar, dialogue from the John Waters film *Polyester*, and the whinnying of horses.

'I had this huge collection of spoken word [and] comedy albums, golf instruction albums, bizarre Christian records,' explained band member Robbie Chater. '[W]e spent a couple a days goofing around and going through the dialogue albums, hanging in my bedroom studio. I remember the records spread out all across my bed and floor and us climbing out the window so we wouldn't disturb the process.'[49]

As Chater suggests, what required The Beatles to take over three studios could be done by The Avalanches decades later in a single bedroom – even if the process was still delicate enough to necessitate defenestration. With the improvement of sampling techniques, they were able to achieve different results too. For instance, while the cuts in 'Revolution 9' are fairly abrupt, The Avalanches could stitch their samples together precisely to create something more musical, so much so that 'Frontier Psychiatrist' became a top twenty hit.[50]

Even so, by drawing on such an eclectic array of samples, the two tracks strike a similar tone – a strange combination of the sinister and the humorous. For 'Frontier Psychiatrist', the dark edge comes through dialogue extracts about mental illness and murder, as well as a dramatic brass and choir motif. But the band undercut this menacing atmosphere with

[49]David James Young, 'The Avalanches Reflect on 20 Years of "Frontier Psychiatrist"', *NME*, 15 October 2020, https://www.nme.com/news/music/the-avalanches-20-year-anniversary-frontier-psychiatrist-2785303.

[50]'Official Charts: The Avalanches', *Official Charts*, https://www.officialcharts.com/artist/7373/avalanches/.

frequent silliness. One sample instructs listeners to 'tighten your buttocks'. And, towards the end of the track, there is an extended turntable scratch solo based around a parrot's squawk.

Though 'Revolution 9' seems more serious at first, it too has comedic undertones. A quiet dialogue extract at the beginning of the track is actually a squabble about a bottle of claret, ending with a muttered insult of 'cheeky bitch'.[51] Likewise, one listener has noted that the track contains 'intermittent shushing, followed almost immediately by the word "it," making shit'.[52]

This balance between the sinister and silly speaks to an essential truth about plunderphonics – that the feeling each sample evokes can be changed based on what it's placed next to. 'This is the essence of creativity to me,' Chater said. 'Joining the dots between unrelated elements [and] showing people the hidden connections.'[53]

In this way, plunderphonics shares a common credo with musique concrète – that no sound is set in stone. Every piece of recorded material contains endless possibilities, either through physically manipulating the audio, or by placing it in a new and surprising setting.

So, whether you are digging through the EMI library or a record shop bargain bin, those sounds contain infinite potential. 'I am reminded of how simple things can be when

[51] Lewisohn, 162.

[52] Tony Sokol, 'The Beatles: In Defense of Revolution 9', *Den of Geek*, 19 September 2019, https://www.denofgeek.com/culture/the-beatles-in-defense-of-revolution-9/.

[53] Young.

making your art,' Chater said, reflecting on 'Frontier Psychiatrist' years later. 'All you really need is a bunch of junkstore records and your imagination.'[54]

For your recommended listening experience, please pair:

'Revolution 9' by The Beatles, 1968 (8:22)
with
'Frontier Psychiatrist' by The Avalanches, 2000 (4:47)

[54]Young.

9 Bernard Parmegiani and acousmatic music

Although musique concrète continued to draw interest from studios and artists, Pierre Schaeffer's strict doctrine could be off-putting. So, in 1974, a new term for the genre was coined by François Bayle, a key member of the *Groupe de Recherches Musicales* (Musical Research Group, or GRM): acousmatic music.[1]

This new title drew on the ancient Greek term *akousmatikoi*, meaning 'those who hear'. It was a word associated with the philosopher Pythagoras, who liked to deliver his lectures from behind a curtain. This curious habit meant his students were forced to focus entirely on his voice, without the distraction of his physical form. For Schaeffer, this captured what he was trying to achieve with his musical experiments and theory: a separation between sounds and their sources.[2]

This new term would often be used synonymously with 'musique concrète'.[3] But it was technically broader, encompassing a greater range of sound sources and treatments.[4] Schaeffer

---

[1] Évelyne Gayou, *A Revolution in Music: The History of the Groupe de Recherches Musicales*, trans. David Vaughn (Berkeley: University of California Press, 2025), 48.
[2] Mark Katz, *Music and Technology: A Very Short Introduction* (Oxford: Oxford University Press, 2022), 21.
[3] Thom Holmes, *Electronic and Experimental Music: Technology, Music, and Culture*, sixth edition (New York: Routledge, 2020), 8.
[4] Thom Holmes, 'Crosscurrents of Musique Concrète', *ThomHolmes.com*, 7 May 2023, https://www.thomholmes.com/post/crosscurrents-of-musique-concr%C3%A8te.

defined the acousmatic as 'referring to a sound that one hears without seeing the causes behind it'.[5] Thus, any music composed for presentation through speakers, rather than live performance, could be considered acousmatic.

Previously, such compositions would have been confined to experimental institutions, like Schaeffer's own GRM. But, as the 1970s loomed, the acousmatic approach was becoming increasingly common in popular music, as the creative process moved from stage to studio.

Experimental rock band the United States of America were early pioneers in this domain. Their first and only album was released in 1968, featuring songs peppered with 'musique concrete-style [*sic*] tape collages'.[6] To recreate this sound onstage, the band became one of the first to incorporate 'not just electronic sound, but whole tape collages' into their shows.[7] For these concerts, tape decks played alongside the band's instrumentals and vocals, creating a combination of acousmatic and live performance.[8]

Another band to experiment with this mix was Pink Floyd. In 1970, they released a studio track, titled 'Alan's

---

[5]FACT Team, 'A Guide to Pierre Schaeffer, the Godfather of Sampling', *Vinyl Factory*, 27 May 2016, https://thevinylfactory.com/features/introduction-to-pierre-schaeffer/.

[6]Cameron Macdonald, 'United States of America, United States of America', *Pitchfork*, 18 October 2004, https://pitchfork.com/reviews/albums/8385-united-states-of-america/.

[7]Simon Reynolds, 'Synthedelia: Psychedelic Electronic Music in the 1960s', *Red Bull Music Academy*, 2 May 2018, https://daily.redbullmusicacademy.com/2018/05/synthedelia.

[8]Klemen Breznikar, 'The United States of America | Joseph Byrd | Interview', *It's Psychedelic Baby! Magazine*, 9 February 2013, https://www.psychedelicbabymag.com/2013/02/joseph-byrd-interview.html.

Psychedelic Breakfast'. This eccentric piece alternated between instrumentals and sound collage segments, which featured the titular Alan discussing, making and eating his morning meal. However, when Pink Floyd tried to reproduce the piece live, they opted to create the sounds organically, with '[e]ggs beaten and fried onstage'.[9] This theatrical performance was abandoned after only four attempts.[10] On later songs, the band would take a more acousmatic approach. For instance, live performances of their song 'Money' saw the band play along with a rhythmic tape loop of clattering coins.[11]

Even bands that were ostensibly less experimental started to produce acousmatic tracks. Creedence Clearwater Revival were known for their steadfast and unpretentious dedication to American Southern-flavoured rock. But in 1970, they issued an experimental single titled '45 Revolutions Per Minute'. Using tape manipulations and sound effects, it aimed to 'get across the elusive Creedence humor'.[12] Listening to it today, that humour remains elusive. But the single nonetheless demonstrates just how far the influence of sound collage, musique concrète and acousmatic music had spread. Even roots rock could not escape it.

But by this point the influence was also flowing in the other direction, as acousmatic composers started to inject popular music into their works. Schaeffer's former protégé,

---

[9] Pink Floyd, *Allen's Psychedelic Breakfast: Pink Floyd, 22 December, Sheffield City Hall, Sheffield* [LP liner notes], unofficial bootleg release.
[10] Andrew Wild, *Pink Floyd: Song By Song* (Fonthill Media Limited, 2017), 55.
[11] Mark Blake, *Pigs Might Fly: The Inside Story of Pink Floyd*, updated and extended paperback edition (London: Aurum Press, 2013), 185.
[12] Creedence Clearwater Revival, *Pendulum: 40th Anniversary Edition* [CD liner notes], Fantasy Records, 2008.

Pierre Henry, created 'an electronic rock ballet' in 1967.[13] One of the tracks, 'Psyché Rock', was even issued as a single.[14] Henry also collaborated with blues-rock band Spooky Tooth. He recruited the group to write and record music, to which he added experimental sounds to create 'an electronic Catholic Mass'. But the project ended in disaster. 'In 1970, the album was released and it tanked', Spooky Tooth member Gary Wright remembered. He believes the project was responsible for destroying the band's career. 'That singular decision took the wind out of our sails,' he recalled. 'Group morale was at an all-time low.'[15]

Some less career-ending attempts to fuse acousmatic and popular music came from composer Bernard Parmegiani. By 1969, he had started to incorporate samples from rock songs into his acousmatic pieces. For his composition 'Pop'eclectic', Parmegiani lifted a bassline from the Pink Floyd song 'Let There Be More Light' and an extract from a track by the Small Faces.[16] Another piece, 'Du pop à l'âne', recycled the Pink Floyd sample, while also adding a prominent section from 'When the Music's Over' by The Doors.[17]

---

[13]Thom Holmes, 'Early Intersections of Rock and Electronic Music', *ThomHolmes.com*, 23 April 2023, https://www.thomholmes.com/post/early-intersections-of-rock-and-electronic-music.

[14]'Les Yper-Sound – Too Fortiche / Psyché Rock', *Discogs*, https://www.discogs.com/master/492527-Les-Yper-Sound-Too-Fortiche-Psych%C3%A9-Rock.

[15]Gary Wright, *Dream Weaver: Music, Meditation, and my Friendship with George Harrison* (New York: Jeremy P. Tarcher/Penguin, 2014), 62.

[16]Oregano Rathbone, 'De Natura Sonorum | Bernard Parmegiani', *Record Collector*, 8 October 2013, https://recordcollectormag.com/reviews/album/de-natura-sonorum.

[17]Holmes, 'Early Intersections of Rock and Electronic Music'.

Parmegiani's use of rock and pop was reflective of his broader open-mindedness to all kinds of music. Over his career, he was said to have 'tried his hand at every genre'.[18] And though he was a key member of Schaeffer's GRM, he resisted following any proscribed direction. 'I've always been forging my own path alone,' he once said.[19]

Indeed, Parmegiani's early career direction was quite singular – before joining the GRM he had trained for 3 years as a mime. But, during that same time, he was also becoming intrigued by musique concrète. 'I used to listen to the first pieces by Schaeffer and Henry on the radio every Sunday,' Parmegiani recalled. 'I was very excited by what I heard.'[20] It was Schaeffer himself who finally forced a decision from Parmegiani, telling him, '[Y]ou have to choose between music and mime.'[21] In the end, he chose music, joining the GRM in 1959, one year after Henry's departure.

But mime continued to influence Parmegiani, even as a composer. 'Sometimes, in order to analyse a sound, I act it out by means of gestures,' he once explained. 'It enables me to diagnose sounds and see if I'm comfortable with them.'[22] This eccentric approach enabled Parmegiani to become one of the GRM composers most associated with the new term,

---

[18]'Biography', official website of Bernard Parmegiani, https://bernard-parmegiani.fr/en/itineraire/biographie/.

[19]Évelyne Gayou, 'Mots de l'immédiat', official website of Bernard Parmegiani, https://bernard-parmegiani.fr/en/itineraire/mots-de-limmediat-entretien-entre-bernard-parmegiani-et-evelyne-gayou/.

[20]Rahma Khazam, 'Bernard Parmegiani: Sound Thinking', *The Wire* # 176, October 1998.

[21]Gayou, 'Mots de l'immédiat'.

[22]Khazam.

acousmatic music. As one article summarized, 'Parmegiani led the way in transforming the early, crude experiments in sound manipulation into the rich and creative genre now known as acousmatic music.'[23]

But Parmegiani's success was not only down to his pantomime roots. He also had the advantage of being able to compose at home. 'I was the first at the GRM to buy my own equipment and have my own personal studio,' he later explained.[24] This may not sound particularly remarkable today. But in the 1960s, such technology took up an inordinate amount of space, especially in the small apartments of Paris. As Parmegiani's wife remembered, the composer had to construct a bespoke unit to house his equipment 'which folded out over the bed during the day and which was folded back up at night'. During her pregnancy, she recalled having 'to slide underneath the folding board' for an afternoon nap.[25]

Parmegiani christened this period the 'Era of the Scissors' – so named for the analogue approach that still required him to cut tape by hand. As his wife remembered, it was a time in which 'domestic objects were given a second life as sonic objects'. In one of her husband's compositions, she could identify the distinct tone of 'a large metal salad bowl that my mother had given us for Christmas'. In another, she recognized a 'grating sound' that came 'from the shutters at our house'.[26]

---

[23] Khazam.

[24] Gayou, 'Mots de l'immédiat'.

[25] Claude-Anne Bezombes Parmegiani, 'Bernard's Studios: The Man of Sound', official website of Bernard Parmegiani, May 2016, https://bernard-parmegiani.fr/en/itineraire/les-studios-de-bernard/.

[26] Claude-Anne Bezombes Parmegiani.

The growth of Parmegiani's domestic sound library culminated in the creation of his masterpiece, *De Natura Sonorum* (On the Nature of Sounds), in 1975. As its title might suggest, the composition took an almost Darwinian approach, categorizing sounds as if they were species in a phylogenetic tree. 'I drew up lists of sounds which I classified by shape, substance, color,' Parmegiani explained.[27] 'I placed the sounds as you do letters, one after the other, so as to create forms and sequences.'[28]

The result was 50 minutes of acousmatic textures, spread across twelve movements. These comprised 'concrete sounds, instrument sounds, and synthesiser sounds', carefully woven together.[29] As Parmegiani declared, the 'piece has since become a classic of electroacoustic music.'[30]

But after his masterpiece was completed, Parmegiani began a transition. 'I had to then teach myself how to work with digital devices,' he recalled.[31] The 'Era of Scissors' was ending. And in the 1980s the 'Age of the Mouse' was beginning.[32]

At first, Parmegiani regretted that there were 'sounds which you could create through analogue which you can't even get through digital'. But he also acknowledged the efficiency in working with computers. He stated that one had 'to admit that

[27] Gayou, 'Mots de l'immédiat'.
[28] Khazam.
[29] David Hirst, 'Schaeffer, GRM and their Influence On NES-Tools For Max', in *Proceedings of the Australasian Computer Music Conference 2019* (Melbourne, 2020), 18.
[30] Khazam.
[31] Gayou, 'Mots de l'immédiat'.
[32] Claude-Anne Bezombes Parmegiani.

the artisinal [*sic*] technique with scissors was quite tedious, whereas writing with the mouse is in some way quicker.'[33]

Furthermore, while some analogue sounds were lost, the 'Age of the Mouse' also revealed a new palette of digital audio. In one composition, Parmegiani manipulated synthesiser tones to create 'a new sonic language'. As he recalled, 'The first time it was performed, people said, that's not Parmegiani. But as far as I was concerned, that meant I had been successful and that I still had something left to say.'[34]

The 'Age of the Mouse' also allowed more composers to build home studios for acousmatic experimentation. The equipment may have been bulky at first. But as the years progressed it would slowly shrink. Functions that once required dozens of technical machines were gradually condensed down into singular computer terminals. And the cost of these declined too. According to data from the thirty-eight countries of the Organisation for Economic Co-operation and Development, home computer ownership surpassed 60 per cent in 2006. By 2020, it was over 78 per cent.[35] And so, as computers entered more homes and workplaces, acousmatic composition became possible for almost anyone.

But technological advances weren't the only thing bringing acousmatic sound to the masses. Parmegiani himself also played a role. In addition to his artistic oeuvre, he composed

[33]Gayou, 'Mots de l'immédiat'.
[34]Khazam.
[35]'Access to Computers from Home', Organisation for Economic Co-operation and Development (OECD), https://www.oecd.org/en/data/indicators/access-to-computers-from-home.html?oecdcontrol-43582d6187-var1=OECD.

themes for news and culture programmes on television.[36] He also created music for advertisements, representing major brands like Renault.[37] Parmegiani's works in these commercial domains represented a final leap in the rebranding of musique concrète. What had once been an esoteric subgenre of the avant-garde was now becoming part of the soundtrack to people's daily lives.

Parmegiani's greatest achievement in mass market composition was his audio jingle for the Charles de Gaulle Airport in Paris. Used to introduce terminal announcements, this three-second composition has been described as 'a micro-masterpiece of electronic music'. From 1971 to 2005, the piece was heard by tens of millions of passengers, making it a strong contender for the most widely known composition by any alumnus of the GRM.[38]

Beyond its enormous listenership, Parmegiani's airport jingle seems almost like a symbol for humanity's entry into a new acousmatic age. It's an era in which our ears are confronted with totally unnatural sounds every day: the ping of the supermarket announcement, the shriek of the car alarm, or the electronic ring of the mobile phone. These inorganic noises are often emitted from speakers which we cannot see or no longer notice. And yet these alien sounds, emanating from the ether, do not disturb us. They are now just part of

[36] 'Biography', official website of Bernard Parmegiani.

[37] Holmes, 'Crosscurrents of Musique Concrète'.

[38] Tom Service, 'Festival Carpets London with Electro Wizardry of Bernard Parmegiani', *The Guardian*, 19 March 2014, https://www.theguardian.com/music/musicblog/2014/mar/19/bernard-parmegiani-electro-london-contemporary-music-festival.

our ordinary environment, as natural to us as the sound of a passing train or the twitter of a bird's song.

Perhaps this is not what Pierre Schaeffer had in mind when he adopted the term acousmatic music. But it is an unexpected fulfilment of his prophetic vision – an absolute separation between sounds and their sources in our everyday world.

A concrete pairing: Bernard Parmegiani and The Prodigy & Public Enemy

In French, there is an expression, 'Passer du coq à l'âne'. The literal translation is something like 'to go from the rooster to the donkey'. But its idiomatic meaning is 'to jump subjects' – based on the proposition that roosters and donkeys have little in common.[39]

Bernard Parmegiani was playing on this phrase when he came up with the title for his 1969 composition, 'Du pop à l'âne'. With the inclusion of 'pop', his pun suggested a series of sonic non-sequiturs, jumping from one fragment of mainstream music to another.

In some ways this was an accurate description. Parmegiani's acousmatic piece drew on extracts from some of the biggest bands of the time: Pink Floyd, The Doors and The Mothers of Invention. But rather than just erratically cutting between these popular music samples, Parmegiani layered them with

[39]Bernard Parmegiani, 'Du pop à l'âne', *Maison ONA*, https://maison-ona.com/catalog-0453ONA.

unexpected pairings from classical compositions. 'For instance, I superimposed a fragment of Pink Floyd over an extract from one of Stravinsky's works,' Parmegiani explained. '[I]t really worked – you'd have thought they were made for each other!'[40]

In this way, Parmegiani may have created an early example of the mashup, a kind of music in which two or more existing tracks are blended together, often matching in tempo and key. Mashups proliferated in the 2000s, as the 'Age of the Mouse' enabled digital files and software to support easier audio editing. What made the genre so unique was its accessibility to everyone. And some of the most successful mashups were created by amateur composers, working from their home computers.

One example is Bob Jackson, a student at the University of Sunderland who uploaded a homemade mashup to the internet in 2015. His piece layered a vocal from Public Enemy's hip-hop track 'Shut 'Em Down' over the instrumental 'Stand Up' by electronic dance band The Prodigy. (The latter was itself based on a sample from jazz rock group Manfred Mann Chapter Three.) In typical mashup fashion, the title was arrived at by blending the two sources together to get 'Shut 'Em Up.'[41]

After gaining traction online, Jackson's mashup caught the attention of Liam Howlett, leader of The Prodigy. 'Liam said he really liked what I had done,' Jackson recalled. In fact, the band were so taken with the track that they added it to a new deluxe edition of their latest album, *The Day Is My Enemy*, which had

[40] Khazam.
[41] Stuart Arnold, 'NE Student's Musical "Mash-up" Included on Prodigy Album', *The Northern Echo*, 26 November 2015, https://www.thenorthernecho.co.uk/news/14106343.ne-students-musical-mash-up-included-prodigy-album/.

been released earlier that year. 'When I found out it was on the album I was stunned,' Jackson said.[42]

Following this official release, 'Shut 'Em Up' gained further exposure. Noel Gallagher from Oasis selected it as one of his choice tracks to be aired on BBC Radio.[43] The song appeared in a movie starring Ice Cube,[44] as well as a commercial for Nike.[45] And it served as the theme music for a Showtime documentary series with the appropriately similar title *Shut Up and Dribble*.[46]

All in all, Jackson's mashup received far more attention than Parmegiani's acousmatic pop collage. And to listen to the two tracks back-to-back, one could be forgiven for finding little in common. Parmegiani's piece remains embedded in the avant-garde, while Jackson's is a thumping anthem, tailor-made for club nights or motivational gym sessions.

But in the methods of their making, there are clear lines to be traced between the two works. Parmegiani's delicate tape layering of Pink Floyd and Stravinsky in the 'Era of the Scissors' prefigures Jackson's digital union of Public Enemy and The Prodigy in the 'Age of the Mouse'. And Parmegiani's construction of his unwieldy home studio marks him out as an early ancestor to bedroom producers like Jackson.

---

[42] Arnold.

[43] 'Noel Gallagher's Christmas Party', *BBC Radio 6*, 18 December 2015, https://www.bbc.co.uk/programmes/b06r8m4q.

[44] *Fist Fight* (2017), [Film] Dir. Richie Keen, United States: Warner Bros. Pictures.

[45] Nike, 'Want it All', Wieden+Kennedy, October 2017.

[46] Alexis Gunderson, '*Shut Up and Dribble* Brings Receipts to the History of Race and Politics in the NBA', *Paste Magazine*, 9 November 2018, https://www.pastemagazine.com/tv/shut-up-and-dribble/showtime-shut-up-and-dribble-docuseries-lebron-jam.

So, perhaps the rooster and the donkey have more in common than we thought.

For your recommended listening experience, please pair:

'Du pop à l'âne' by Bernard Parmegiani, 1969 (10:08)
with
'Shut 'Em Up' by The Prodigy & Public Enemy, 2015 (4:20)

10 Beatriz Ferreyra and the last of the concrete legends

Throughout his early experiments with musique concrète, Pierre Schaeffer harboured nagging uncertainties. 'Perhaps concrete music was not music,' he wondered in 1951. 'Perhaps it never would be?'[1]

These doubts lingered. Even towards the end of his life, Schaeffer was still questioning the validity of the genre he had inaugurated. 'I was always deeply unhappy at what I was doing,' he reflected in 1987. '[I]t's not that I disown everything I did – it was a lot of hard work. But each time I was to experience the disappointment of not arriving at music. I couldn't get to music, what I call music.'[2]

Schaeffer's dissatisfaction meant that he didn't define himself by his relationship to musique concrète. 'I have three jobs,' he once said: 'writer, researcher and administrator'. That he listed 'writer' first was telling. It harkened back to his original literary ambitions as an *écrivain*. And he actually had some success in this domain. In 1970, he even won the prestigious

[1] Pierre Schaeffer, *In Search of a Concrete Music*, trans. Christine North & John Dack (Berkeley: University of California Press, 2012), 105.
[2] Thom Holmes, *Electronic and Experimental Music: Technology, Music, and Culture*, sixth edition (New York: Routledge, 2020), 229.

Prix Sainte-Beuve for his third novel, *Le Gardien de Volcan* (The Volcano Guardian).[3]

When Schaeffer passed away in 1995 at age 85, some obituaries recognized the diversity of his achievements. The headline in *Le Monde* declared him 'Neither researcher, nor composer, nor writer'. Instead, he was an 'awakener'.[4] But still, there was no escaping the fact that musique concrète would be his legacy, even if he himself could never quite grasp it. 'I think of myself as an explorer struggling to find a way through the far north,' Schaeffer reflected. '[B]ut I wasn't finding a way through.'[5]

Meanwhile, Schaeffer's erstwhile apprentice, Pierre Henry, seemed more secure in his legacy and the validity of musique concrète. In fact, he converted 'his Paris home into a living musical instrument' devoted to acousmatic projection.[6] He invited audiences inside, playing his tape music for them through a network of thirty-six speakers that penetrated the kitchen, office, library, and beyond. 'One or two people can lie down on the master bed,' one report even claimed.[7] This eccentricity won Henry new fans. 'I feel that my public continues to be a young one,' he stated in 2006.[8] And indeed,

---

[3] 'Media man', *The Times*, 20 April 1970, 8.

[4] A.R., 'Ni chercheur, ni compositeur, ni écrivain: éveilleur', *Le Monde*, 22 August 1995, 16.

[5] Holmes, 229.

[6] Geeta Dayal, 'The Life And Work Of Pierre Henry, Ceaseless Sonic Explorer', *NPR*, 8 July 2017, https://www.npr.org/sections/therecord/2017/07/08/536046909/the-life-and-work-of-pierre-henry-ceaseless-sonic-explorer.

[7] 'Obituary: Pierre Henry', *The Times*, 27 July 2017, https://www.thetimes.com/uk/article/pierre-henry-356dxt6x2.

[8] *Pierre Henry: The Art of Sounds* (2006), [Film] Dir. Franck Mallet & Éric Darmon, France: © Mémoire Magnétique / ARTE France / Love Streams agnès b. Productions.

his 1967 composition 'Psyché Rock' took on a second life at the turn of the century, significantly bolstering his youth appeal.

Firstly, Fatboy Slim remixed Henry's track in 1997. Shortly after, composer Christopher Tyng reinterpreted the song to create the theme music for animated sitcom *Futurama*. A few years later, hip-hop royalty Busta Rhymes used a sample from Henry's original on his track 'What Up'. And finally, in a most unexpected twist, the remixed version of 'Psyché Rock' found its way into the teen movie *Mean Girls* and was even issued on the official soundtrack.

But Henry's cool credentials went beyond this single track. The hip-hop artist D'Angelo used an extract from Henry's 'Jericho Jerk' for his track 'Devil's Pie'. Henry also served as a producer on an album by the American alternative rock band The Violent Femmes.[9] And when he composed a Mass for the Liverpool Metropolitan Cathedral, the piece was introduced by Jarvis Cocker, frontman of the Britpop band Pulp.[10]

This Liverpool Mass would prove to be one of the last presentations of Henry's music during his lifetime. Like Schaeffer, he had devoted himself to searching for an elusive sound. But for Henry, it seemed that the journey was defined more by wonder and fulfilment, rather than the frustrations of his mentor. 'What tempts me is pure sound,' Henry confessed. 'The possibilities of that sound . . . eternal possibilities . . .,' he added, drifting off into thought. 'It's a curse, and yet, it's also extraordinary.'[11]

---

[9]The Violent Femmes, *Freak Magnet* [album], Cooking Vinyl, UK, 2000.
[10]'Obituary', *The Times*.
[11]*Pierre Henry: The Art of Sounds* [Film].

Henry passed away in July 2017 at the age of 89. Schaeffer preceded him in death, as did almost all the other concrete legends. And as they passed through their twilight years, each received some unique recognition. Iannis Xenakis, the surly Greek, became a Knight in the French Legion of Honour, one of the highest forms of recognition his adopted country could give.[12] Bernard Parmegiani was acknowledged as 'possibly the most important figure to have emerged from the Parisian school of electroacoustic composers'.[13] He was also cited as an influence on popular electronic artists like Autechre, who chose him as part of their lineup for a music festival in 2003.[14] As for Tod Dockstader, the American outsider, his works were reissued on CD in the 1990s. This time, the reviews were 'better by far than anything the music ever got in its day'. *The Washington Post* even described him as 'one of the giants in the field'.[15] When he finally passed away in 2015, Dockstader was listening to his own music – peacefully.[16]

Remarkably, despite being the earliest pioneer of the concrete clan, the eccentric Egyptian Halim El-Dabh outlived them all. Over a career that spanned eight decades, he left behind

---

[12]Norma Beecroft, *Conversations With Post World War II Pioneers of Electronic, Music* promotional copy (Canadian Music Centre, 2015), 14.

[13]Roger Sutherland, 'Parmegiani', *London Magazine* 31, no. 11 (1 February 1992): 106.

[14]Ollie Appleby, 'ATP 2003 Sold Out and Lineup Confirmed', *Drowned in Sound*, 20 February 2003, https://drownedinsound.com/news/6162-atp-2003-sold-out-and-lineup-confirmed.

[15]Tom Steenland, 'Remembering Tod Dockstader (1932–2015)', *New Music USA*, 27 March 2015, https://newmusicusa.org/nmbx/remembering-tod-dockstader-1932-2015/.

[16]Zoe Camp, 'Musique Concrète Composer Tod Dockstader Has Died', *Pitchfork*, 27 February 2015, https://pitchfork.com/news/58660-musique-concrete-composer-tod-dockstader-has-died/.

an enormous body of work, encompassing a remarkable diversity. There were 'the haunting, Eastern-infused ballets he wrote';[17] the musical drama he created to memorialise four students killed at Kent State, the university he was affiliated with for almost 50 years;[18] and the orchestral work he composed, which was performed nightly as part of the sound and light show at the Great Pyramids of Giza.[19]

But in those final years, El-Dabh found himself drawn back to his first wire recorder experiments. Thanks to a CD reissue compiling his early works, he was gaining increasing recognition as the originator of musique concrète; in fact, many of his final interviews focused on this detail. But for El-Dabh, his music was all part of a singular tapestry. He once 'asserted that there was really only one tone in the world and that all sounds came from that single pitch, which traveled throughout the universe.'[20]

Even so, when El-Dabh died in September 2017, at the age of 96, it seemed like the end of the concrete era. The Egyptian originator of the genre was gone, as well as the two Pierres who had defined its scope and sound. And almost all their concrete progeny had died too – from Karlheinz Stockhausen to Luc Ferrari.

[17] Margalit Fox, 'Halim El-Dabh, Composer of Martha Graham Ballets, Dies at 96', *New York Times*, 8 September 2017, https://www.nytimes.com/2017/09/08/arts/music/halim-el-dabh-dies.html.
[18] '1995 Commemoration: Opera Flies by Halim El-Dabh', Kent State University Libraries. Special Collections and Archives, http://omeka.library.kent.edu/special-collections/items/show/4494.
[19] Fox.
[20] Denise A. Seachrist, *The Musical World of Halim El-Dabh* (Kent: The Kent State University Press, 2003), 19.

But in the midst of this final decline, one concrete legend reemerged: Beatriz Ferreyra. She had been a member of Schaeffer's *Groupe de Recherches Musicales* (Musical Research Group, or GRM) in the 1960s.[21] As one of the only female composers of the time, her work had been somewhat overlooked. But as she entered her ninth decade of life, she would finally bring her works to a wider audience, sounding a last coda for musique concrète.

Ferreyra was born in Córdoba, Argentina in 1937. She grew up surrounded by music, studying piano and violin. 'I think that all the music I heard in my childhood made me discover something very flexible and unique in sound,' she later reflected. '[B]ut as a child I didn't compose. It was not something I did.'[22]

Her creative urges were kindled later, when she moved to Paris. Initially pursuing a career as a painter, her life changed when Argentinian composer Edgardo Cantón took her to a concert of electro-acoustic music in 1963. 'I developed a real interest in *musique concrète*,' Ferreyra recalled. 'I said to Edgardo that I had to write this kind of music, and he introduced me to Schaeffer.'[23]

After completing 'a short residency in Schaeffer's studio', she was admitted to the GRM in 1964.[24] For much of her time there

[21] 'Biography', official website of Beatriz Ferreyra, https://beatrizferreyra.odexpo.com/default.asp?page=41341&sm=41352&lg=.
[22] Kim S. Courchene, 'A Conversation with Beatriz Ferreyra', *Computer Music Journal* 25, no. 3 (2001): 14.
[23] Courchene, 15.
[24] Courchene, 15.

she was the only female composer working with Schaeffer.[25] But she became a trusted member of his team, contributing to the ambitious music theory he was formulating during the 1960s. Even decades later, she continued to describe sounds using Schaefferian terms, such as *impulsions* (sharp attacks) and *percutés* (percussive hits).[26]

Although Schaeffer was alienating certain members of the GRM at this time, Ferreyra found his influence profound. 'He opened Pandora's box,' she said. 'Every sound of nature – of the whole universe – could be transformed into a musical sound [. . .] This was for me a real revolution.'[27]

Ferreyra was especially inspired by Schaeffer's perspective on the act of hearing. 'We learned, in electro-acoustic music with Schaeffer, to change our point of view, to hear something which is a sound and not that which produced the sound,' Ferreyra summarized. 'I don't know how others do music, but I do music with this other kind of hearing.'[28]

Certain members of the GRM found Schaeffer's theories restrictive to the creative process. But for Ferreyra, the musique concrète palette offered endless possibilities. 'It has no limits,' she said. 'It has no rules. And it's infinite.'[29] Her sense of artistic freedom came across in interviews. As well as the technical

[25]'Beatriz Ferreyra & Christine Groult', *ISSUE* [concert event description], 2019, https://issueprojectroom.org/event/beatriz-ferreyra-christine-groult.
[26]Beatriz Ferreyra, *Huellas Entreveradas* [LP liner notes], Persistence of Sound, 2020.
[27]Courchene, 15.
[28]'Acousmonium: INA grm – Groupe de Recherches Musicales', *MaerzMusik* [concert programme booklet], 15 March 2024, 9.
[29]'Beatriz Ferreyra', *NTS* [radio interview], 30 April 2024, https://www.nts.live/shows/guests/episodes/beatriz-ferreyra-30th-april-2024.

Schaefferian terms, she was also fond of describing sounds through her own invented onomatopoeic words, such as 'schkllang, prrrrwip, ferrrwisssssh [and] takatak'.[30]

Ferreyra's first composition at the GRM was a 3-minute student piece, completed in 1965. After that, she was commissioned to produce three more works between 1968 and 1970. These premiered at festivals in France and on the radio.[31] But, unlike many of her GRM contemporaries, Ferreyra's works never had a wide release on record.

After leaving the GRM in 1970, much of Ferreyra's subsequent output was equally obscure. She cited her work on a strange Italian art film, *Homo Sapiens*, as one of her more significant projects. Directed by Fiorella Mariani (niece of cinematic auteur Roberto Rossellini), the film is 'made up of footage selected without any concern for place, time and ideology'. It featured Ferreyra's acousmatic sounds over the top of this visual melange.[32] 'This was a very important experience for me, because I wrote an entire hour of electroacoustic music,' Ferreyra said.[33]

Alongside commissions like these, Ferreyra also found a place in academia. But she noticed a change in her students as tape machines gradually made way for computers. 'I now see young composers "looking" at the sound in front of them,' she said in 2001, referring to the waveforms on their monitors.

---

[30] *Huellas Entreveradas* [LP liner notes].
[31] 'Works', official website of Beatriz Ferreyra, https://beatrizferreyra.odexpo.com/default.asp?page=41340&sm=41353&lg=.
[32] 'Homo sapiens, a film by Fiorella Mariani', *Nomadica* [film description], https://www.nomadica.eu/homo-sapiens/.
[33] Courchene, 17–18.

In the GRM days, Ferreyra noted, 'We did not see a waveform in front of us. We worked only on hearing the sounds.' While she acknowledged that the onscreen innovation was 'very practical for editing', she also asserted that it was 'a trap for the ears'. She tried to pull her students back to the Schaefferian way of hearing. But it was in vain. 'I just turn their chairs away from the computer, and many of them simply become lost,' she explained.[34]

Ferreyra eventually accepted the inevitability of the 'Age of the Mouse'. She even began composing on Pro Tools herself, using digital software to replicate the old GRM techniques. At first, she referred to her computer as 'this terrible machine'.[35] And she held onto her antique Revox tape recorders for 'techniques that can't be achieved with computer software'.[36] But eventually, she admitted, 'I prefer the computer because it is easier'.[37]

And so, as the old techniques of working with tape faded away, it seemed as if the era of musique concrète was over. But it was just in this twilight moment that Ferreyra's earlier tape works suddenly experienced a resurgence – giving her long-overdue recognition as a key member of the GRM, and sounding a poignant final note for the story of musique concrète.

[34] Courchene, 17.
[35] Courchene, 19.
[36] *Huellas Entreveradas* [LP liner notes].
[37] Geeta Dayal, 'Beatriz Ferreyra: Making Music with All the Sounds in the World', *National Sawdust*, 21 February 2018, https://www.nationalsawdust.org/thelog/2018-02-21-beatriz-ferreyra-making-music-with-all-the-sounds-in-the-world.

The catalyst for this was a CD compilation released in 2015, which issued two of Ferreyra's 1960s GRM works for the first time, alongside a pair of newer compositions.[38] Soon after, she found herself on the bill at the Semibreve Festival in Portugal.[39] She then performed in Berlin[40] and London,[41] and made her United States debut at the age of 80.[42]

But Ferreyra's biggest exposure came in 2020, when she released another album, *Echos+*. Like the previous compilation, it coupled unreleased tape works from Ferreyra's archive with newer compositions. But it was the musique concrète title track – which had its origins half a century earlier – that garnered the most attention.

The sound source for this composition came from a niece of Ferreyra's, who visited her in Paris in the 1970s. 'I didn't know her,' Ferreyra recalled. 'She was twenty years old, or twenty-two or eighteen – I don't remember. And she told me that she wanted to be a singer.'[43] When the young niece gave a

[38] Andy Beta, 'GRM Works / Pacific Tubular Waves / Immersion', *Pitchfork*, 8 May 2015, https://pitchfork.com/reviews/albums/20526-grm-works-pacific-tubular-wavesimmersion/.
[39] Eoin Murray, 'Things Learned At: Semibreve Festival', *The Quietus*, 3 November 2017, https://thequietus.com/quietus-reviews/live-reviews/semibreve-portugal-beatriz-ferreyra/.
[40] 'Portrait #09 Beatriz Ferreyra – German Premiere', *Heroines of Sound Festival*, 2018, https://www.heroines-of-sound.com/editions-2018/#edition-2-beatriz-ferreyra.
[41] 'Beatriz Ferreyra (live) + Eliane Radigue & Alison Knowles performed by Angharad Davies / Rhodri Davies / Dominic Lash + films by Holly Antrum and Keira Greene', *Café Oto*, 2019, https://www.cafeoto.co.uk/events/beatriz-ferreyra-eliane-radigue-alison-knowles/.
[42] 'Beatriz Ferreyra & Christine Groult', *Issue Project Room*, 2019, https://issueprojectroom.org/event/beatriz-ferreyra-christine-groult.
[43] *NTS* [radio interview].

demonstration, Ferreyra took out her tape recorder to capture the Latin American tunes she sang.[44]

Four or 5 years later, Ferreyra received the tragic news that her niece had been killed in a motor accident.[45] Returning to the tapes, Ferreyra decided to create a tribute to her lost relative. She used 'techniques of tape cutting, mixing and manual shakes' to construct her 8-minute composition.[46] In the finished piece, the melodies were warped beyond recognition. But the voice sang in new ways.

When it was finally released in 2020, the track garnered an almost unprecedented amount of attention for a musique concrète work. Most notably, it was named one of the top 100 songs of the year by *Pitchfork*. The reviewer declared that listening to the track was akin to 'stumbling upon a roadside shrine of flowers'.[47] This comment might have referred to Ferreyra's niece. But it could just as easily have applied to musique concrète itself – by this point a dying genre, memorialized one last time by Ferreyra's poignant composition. Several years later, at the mid-point of the decade, 'Echos' was again cited by *Pitchfork* – this time as one of the 100 best songs of the 2020s. Ferreyra's touching track was placed at a respectable number eighty-two, positioned somewhat awkwardly next to a song called 'Fuck Him All Night' by Azealia Banks.[48]

---

[44] 'Works', official website of Beatriz Ferreyra.
[45] *NTS* [radio interview].
[46] 'Works', official website of Beatriz Ferreyra.
[47] 'The 100 Best Songs of 2020', *Pitchfork*, 7 December 2020, https://pitchfork.com/features/lists-and-guides/best-songs-2020/.
[48] 'The 100 Best Songs of the 2020s So Far', *Pitchfork*, 30 September 2024, https://pitchfork.com/features/lists-and-guides/the-100-best-songs-of-the-2020s-so-far/.

In the wake of this success, Ferreyra released another album in 2021 and two more in 2023. These attracted coverage in the popular press, with reviews in *Pitchfork*[49] and *The Guardian*,[50] as well as radio play on the BBC.[51] One reviewer described the music as having 'a curious beauty'. And Ferreyra herself was heralded as 'the last surviving member from the field of mid-20th-century pioneers that included the likes of Edgard Varèse and Pierre Henry'.[52]

Perhaps it was this status as the last of the concrete legends that maintained her drive to keep creating well beyond any normal retirement age. Indeed, many of her later works paid tribute to the other pioneers of the past, such as Bernard Parmegiani.[53] But she was also sending a signal to the next generation.

'They don't know that they have an infinite possibility to do an infinite music with infinite sounds,' she said in 2024. 'Electro-acoustic music is free. It has no limits. It's composing with all the sounds in the world,' she added. 'But you must learn to hear them.'[54]

---

[49] Joshua Minsoo Kim, 'Senderos de luz y sombras, Beatriz Ferreyra', *Pitchfork*, 6 January 2023, https://pitchfork.com/reviews/albums/beatriz-ferreyra-senderos-de-luz-y-sombras/.

[50] John Lewis, 'Beatriz Ferreyra: Canto+ Review – Painterly Daubs of Found Sound', *The Guardian*, 30 July 2021, https://www.theguardian.com/music/2021/jul/30/beatriz-ferreyra-canto-review-musique-concrete.

[51] 'The City, Full of People', *BBC Radio 3: New Music Show*, 25 November 2023, https://www.bbc.co.uk/programmes/m001slz1.

[52] Lewis.

[53] Andy Beta, 'Huellas Entreveradas, Beatriz Ferreyra', *Pitchfork*, 8 May 2020, https://pitchfork.com/reviews/albums/beatriz-ferreyra-huellas-entreveradas/.

[54] *NTS* [radio interview].

A concrete pairing: Beatriz Ferreyra and The Beatles

What happens to our voices when we die? For centuries, spiritual mediums have claimed to have the answer – from the blind *itako* women of Japan,[55] to the seance leaders of Victorian England.[56] But, when Beatriz Ferreyra composed 'Echos' in 1978, she suggested the occult might be accessed through technology rather than spiritualism.

For Ferreyra, the voice she wished to resurrect belonged to her niece, whose singing she had captured a few years before the young woman's death. And to make her speak again, Ferreyra applied the techniques of musique concrète, carving a new song from her niece's voice. 'I did "Echos" so she can continue to sing,' Ferreyra simply said.[57]

When the track was finally released in 2020, one reviewer compared this renewed vocal to a communication with the afterlife. 'Her voice seems to carry from a great distance—not just across years, but dimensions,' he wrote. 'In its haunting frequencies, we glimpse the outline of the afterworld.'[58] But by that time, new technologies were taking the paranormal idea Ferreyra had laid down on tape even further. One innovation,

[55] Martin Fackler, 'As Japan's Mediums Die, Ancient Tradition Fades', *New York Times*, 20 August 2009, 8.
[56] Casey Cep, 'Why Did So Many Victorians Try to Speak with the Dead?', *The New Yorker*, 24 May 2021, https://www.newyorker.com/magazine/2021/05/31/why-did-so-many-victorians-try-to-speak-with-the-dead.
[57] *NTS* [radio interview].
[58] Philip Sherburne, 'Echos, Beatriz Ferreyra', 18 March 2020, https://pitchfork.com/reviews/tracks/beatriz-ferreyra-echos/.

which involved artificial intelligence (AI), was even about to resurrect The Beatles.

The band had split in 1970. Though rumours of a reconciliation had persisted for years, John Lennon's death in 1980 ended the speculation. 'When we lost John, we knew that it was really over,' Paul McCartney said.[59] Despite this, the surviving members came together a decade later, completing two songs Lennon had left behind as demos – 'Free As a Bird' and 'Real Love'. A third song, titled 'Now and Then', was attempted. But it proved impossible. Lennon had demoed it on a home cassette recorder, fusing his voice and piano to a single track, with the instrument often drowning out his singing.[60]

However, by the 2020s, machine learning had become powerful enough for these sounds to be separated. Producer Giles Martin offered a colourful metaphor to illustrate how remarkable the technology was. 'It's like you giving me a cake, and then me going back to you about an hour later with flour, eggs, sugar, and all the ingredients,' he explained.[61]

With this new innovation, 'Now and Then' could be attempted again. 'We could strip back the opening of the song

---

[59] *The Beatles - Now And Then - The Last Beatles Song (Short Film)* (2023), [Film] Dir. Oliver Murray, United Kingdom: Orofena Films.

[60] *The Beatles - Now And Then - The Last Beatles Song (Short Film).*

[61] Rob Sheffield, 'The Beatles' Unheard "Revolver": An Exclusive Preview of a Blockbuster Archival Release', *Rolling Stone*, 7 September 2022, https://www.rollingstone.com/music/music-features/the-beatles-revolver-unheard-archives-sheffield-1234587264/.

and have John on his own, separated from the piano,' Martin explained. 'And it's unmistakably John Lennon.'[62]

McCartney's reaction to this isolated vocal conjured images of a man brought back from the dead. 'When we were in the studio, we had John's voice in our ears so you could imagine he was just in the next room,' he recalled.[63]

To complete the track, McCartney and drummer Ringo Starr added an instrumental backing. Martin arranged a string section. George Harrison, who had died in 2001, was also represented through a guitar part he had recorded in the 1990s.

But Lennon's AI-extracted voice was the centrepiece, which seemed appropriate given his experimental leanings. 'My dad would have loved that because he was never shy to experiment with recording technology,' Lennon's son Sean said of the finished song. 'I think it's really beautiful.'[64]

The track was positively received upon its 2023 release and even became the first AI-assisted song to be nominated at the Grammys,[65] picking up a nod for Record of the Year and a win for Best Rock Performance.[66]

---

[62] Rob Sheffield, 'The Beatles Return for One More Masterpiece With New Song "Now and Then"', *Rolling Stone*, 2 November 2023, https://www.rollingstone.com/music/music-news/beatles-new-song-now-and-then-1234868643/.

[63] Mark Savage, 'The Beatles' Last Song Now and Then is Finally Released', *BBC News*, 2 November 2023, https://www.bbc.co.uk/news/entertainment-arts-67285117.

[64] *The Beatles - Now And Then - The Last Beatles Song (Short Film).*

[65] Kristin Robinson, 'The Beatles' "Now and Then" Makes History As First AI-Assisted Song to Earn Grammy Nomination', *Billboard*, 8 November 2024, https://www.billboard.com/pro/the-beatles-now-and-then-first-ai-assisted-song-grammy-nomination-history/.

[66] Nina Frazier, '2025 GRAMMYs: See The Full Winners & Nominees List', *Grammy Awards*, 3 February 2025, https://www.grammy.com/news/2025-grammys

But there was trepidation from some fans about the use of AI. Many assumed generative software had been used to synthesize Lennon's voice.[67] McCartney even issued a statement to clarify how the technology worked. 'We've seen some confusion and speculation about it,' he said. '[T]o be clear, nothing has been artificially or synthetically created.'[68]

Like Ferreyra's work with 'Echos', the new Beatles track was only using the raw material of the original voice. Still, it seemed to gesture towards a future where the voices of the dead could be made again in a different way – and forced to speak words they would never have uttered in life. Indeed, around the time 'Now and Then' was announced, the internet was becoming awash with frivolous AI-produced acts of resurrection, such as an artificial Frank Sinatra singing the Oasis hit 'Wonderwall'.[69]

Just a year after 'Now and Then' was released, McCartney even started warning about such technologies. 'I think AI is great,' he clarified. 'But it shouldn't rip creative people off. There's no sense in that.'[70] By 2025, he had released a track protesting a proposed UK law, which would allow companies to train their AI products using the copyrighted work of musicians. (Interestingly, McCartney's protest track had

-nominations-full-winners-nominees-list.

[67] Robinson.

[68] Michael Sun, 'Paul McCartney Says There's Nothing Artificial in New Beatles Song Made Using AI', *The Guardian*, 23 June 2023, https://www.theguardian.com/music/2023/jun/23/paul-mccartney-says-theres-nothing-artificial-in-new-beatles-song-made-using-ai.

[69] Daisy Jones, 'AI Cover Songs from Dead Musicians are Morbid, Exploitative and Tacky as Hell', *GQ*, 23 August 2023, https://www.gq-magazine.co.uk/article/dead-musiciains-ai-generated-songs.

[70] Laura Kuenssberg, 'Paul McCartney: Don't let AI Rip Off Artists', *BBC News*, 25 January 2025, https://www.bbc.co.uk/news/articles/c8xqv9g8442o.

something of a musique concrète feel. It included no singing or instrumentation – to represent the silencing of musicians – and instead consisted of tape hiss, clattering noises and the sound of a door opening.)[71]

For McCartney and Ferreyra, their musical mediumship had sought to bring back long-dead voices in a loving, respectful way. But now a new future loomed, in which the dark art of resurrection was revealed to anyone savvy enough to download a bit of open-source AI software. From this point forward, the voices of the dead could never rest peacefully again. With just a few seconds of audio,[72] any voice could be brought back to life and manipulated into speaking anything, with no will of its own: a warning, perhaps, on the dangers of playing with the occult.

For your recommended listening experience, please pair:

'Echos' by Beatriz Ferreyra, 2020 (8:33)
with
'Now and Then' by The Beatles, 2023 (4:08)

[71] Robert Booth, 'Paul McCartney Joins Music Industry Protest Against AI with Silent Track', *The Guardian*, 17 November 2025, https://www.theguardian.com/music/2025/nov/17/the-sound-of-silence-why-theres-barely-anything-there-in-paul-mccartney-new-release.

[72] James Tyrrell, 'Microsoft Shaves Voice Cloning Time Down to 3 Seconds', *Tech HQ*, 12 January 2023, https://techhq.com/2023/01/microsoft-shaves-voice-cloning-time-down-to-3-seconds/.

Epilogue

Whatever happened to musique concrète?

There is nothing to stop anyone from making musique concrète today. In fact, in many ways, it is easier to create than ever. The tyranny of the 'Era of the Scissors' is over. One no longer needs access to exclusive studios or expensive equipment. In the digital age, recorded sound can now be captured, manipulated, edited and disseminated all on a single device.

Some of the old concrete studios even offer software to help composers recreate the sounds and techniques of the analogue age. For instance, you can buy a digital library of 'treasure-trove tape archives' from the BBC Radiophonic Workshop.[1] Pierre Schaeffer's old studio also offers a series of digital plugins, known as GRM Tools.[2]

But can a composition truly be described as musique concrète if it is made entirely by digital means? Such an approach seems to go against the original tenets of the genre, which placed physical recording devices as the instruments of composition. Halim El-Dabh hinted at this when he described

---

[1] Spitfire Audio, 'BBC Radiophonic Workshop', 2025, https://www.spitfireaudio.com/bbc-radiophonic-workshop.

[2] Sam Inglis, 'INA GRM Tools 3', *Sound on Sound*, September 2011, https://www.soundonsound.com/reviews/ina-grm-tools-3.

his process with a sculpting analogy. 'I was carving sound,' he said. 'I used noise like I would a piece of stone.'[3] Schaeffer landed on the same metaphor, referring to his sound material as 'unworked stone'.[4]

Indeed, there is something about musique concrète that implies touch. Being able to hold a piece of sound in your hands is central to the art. Hence that word – concrete – which suggests something that exists in tactile, material form.

Perhaps then, musique concrète is not a genre at all. Rather, it is a way of exploring sound. And that 'way' is inherently tied to physical media – phonograph records, wire recorders and magnetic tape. These archaic technologies are now vanishing into obsolescence. A handful of eccentric composers may continue to preserve them as long as possible: artists like Robin the Fog, Jérôme Noetinger, and the Japanese band Open Reel Ensemble have all produced tape music well into the digital age. But as the machines for composition inevitably cease being manufactured and fall into disrepair, with no spare parts to replace them, the art of traditional musique concrète necessarily dies too.

But even as musique concrète in its true form fades into the past, its legacy lives on. As music historian Thom Holmes notes:

> Software designed for the editing and processing of sounds continues to borrow its lexicon of terms and controls from the

[3] Margalit Fox, 'Halim El-Dabh, Composer of Martha Graham Ballets, Dies at 96,' *New York Times*, 8 September 2017, https://www.nytimes.com/2017/09/08/arts/music/halim-el-dabh-dies.html.

[4] Pierre Schaeffer, *In Search of a Concrete Music*, trans. Christine North & John Dack (University of California Press, 2012), 19.

world of magnetic tape, where the concepts of Record, Play, Fast Forward, Rewind, and Pause were first applied.[5]

Likewise, many techniques that originated in the concrete studios continue to proliferate in popular music. These include sampling, looping, pitch transposition, superimposing sounds, mashups, and more. Other ideas, like Iannis Xenakis' pioneering work with microsounds, can now be taken further – as digital technologies allow sounds to be sliced into fragments smaller than any scissors could manage.

So, the concrete legends leave a legacy. But the transition of their techniques from physical media to the digital realm only underscores the death of their methodology. What was once grounded in the physical world, now exists in an ethereal cybernetic space – where sounds can be heard but never quite grasped. This mirrors the way things were before recording technologies existed. Back then, sounds would briefly float like spectres on the air before disappearing into the void forever. In the digital age, sounds can at least be played back. But, in some ways, they are more ghostly than ever. They live in stasis in some invisible electronic mainframe, only to be called up like spirits at our command.

The lifespan of musique concrète exists somewhere between those two points of the pre-recording era and the digital age. It was a brief moment in which sound was pulled from its ethereal state to become a physical object. One could trace one's fingers through a moment in time captured in the

[5]Thom Holmes, *Electronic and Experimental Music: Technology, Music, and Culture*, sixth edition (New York: Routledge, 2020), 108.

grooves of a wax cylinder or phonograph disc. And one could measure out seconds or minutes of sound by pulling a length of wire or tape through one's hands.

Physical media existed as the dominant recording form for only a little over a century. And musique concrète was at its apex for less than half of that. It's a remarkably human lifespan – and infinitesimally small within the context of music history. But its significance exceeds its brevity. Because it was the only moment in human existence when sound became solid, when you could hold a piece of time in your hands – when music was concrete.

Acknowledgements

The story of musique concrète is a tale of contrasts, encompassing both lone composers (like Halim El-Dabh and Tod Dockstader) as well as serial collaborators (like Pierre Henry and Luc Ferrari). Writing a book mirrors these extremes. There are long periods typing away in isolation. And there are pivotal moments of collaboration, without which nothing would happen.

First, I must thank my friend Greg Stall – a man of unsurpassed musical knowledge! It was my conversations with Greg which gave me the initial push to submit a proposal to 33 1/3, setting the wheels in motion for the genesis of this strange book. Thank you, Greg, for that first spark of inspiration, as well as your continued interest in, and encouragement for, this esoteric project.

Next, I must express my gratitude to Leah Babb-Rosenfeld, who leads the 33 1/3 team at Bloomsbury. She considered my initial proposal (a treatise on the musical career of William Shatner) with good humour, before prodding me in the direction of the Genre series and offering kind words of encouragement along the way.

Once settled on the subject of musique concrète, I was fortunate to have one of the best professionals in the publishing business to look over my proposal: Eleanor Christie. Thank you, Elli – your cromulent suggestions truly embiggened that document!

After many months of toil, I was lucky to have another great editor come onboard to review the manuscript: Annie Zaleski, aka the hardest working music writer in the business (in the time it took me to complete this one book, I think she released four or five). Thank you, Annie, for your generous praise, as well as your gentle critiques!

I would also like to thank everyone on the team at Bloomsbury who worked on this book – Alex Sobrino, Elena Durey and Emma Leask. There's a lot that goes into turning a simple Word document into a polished and professional product. So I'm truly grateful for all your support with production, design and everything else that makes a finished book.

Finally, I'd like to thank my parents for raising me in a house full of books – now here's one more to add to the shelf!

10 essential tracks

1. **Halim El-Dabh, 'Wire Recorder Piece' (1944, released 2000) [1:58]**
   When Halim El-Dabh premiered 'The Expression of Zaar' as a sound installation in 1944, it lasted 20 to 25 minutes. This 2-minute extract was given a wider release in 2000. As the only fragment we have from that earliest work of musique concrète, it's essential listening for any student of the genre.
2. **Pierre Schaeffer & Pierre Henry, 'Apostrophe' (1950) [2:22]**
   Pierre Schaeffer and Pierre Henry's collaborative opus *Symphonie pour un homme seul* exists in different versions. Depending on which you find, this track is either the eighth or ninth movement. But listen to the entire symphony (around 20 minutes) for a more complete concrete experience.
3. **Pierre Henry, 'Vagues' (1963) [1:36]**
   Like the above entry, this track is just one part of a larger work. In this case, it's the nineteenth movement from Pierre Henry's *Variations pour une porte et un soupir.* The entire work lasts around 48 minutes. It's worth a listen if you're intrigued to hear the full gamut of sounds Henry extracts from his titular *porte* (door) and *soupir* (sigh).

4. **Iannis Xenakis, 'Concret PH' (1958) [2:45]**
   This short piece was played for visitors to the Philips Pavilion at the 1958 Brussels World's Fair during changeovers between performances. Equally essential is Edgard Varèse's 8-minute *Poème électronique*, which provided the soundtrack to the main show.
5. **Luc Ferrari, 'Presque Rien n°1' (1970) [20:46]**
   This pioneering piece emerged following Luc Ferrari's 8 years at the GRM. But it's arguably not a work of musique concrète at all. Rather, it's a transitional composition, showcasing how musique concrète was evolving and converging with the genre of soundscapes. Ferrari said that it contained his '[f]irst conceptions about minimalism'.
6. **Tod Dockstader, 'Water Music, Pt. Two' (1963) [2:56]**
   Like other essential tracks on this list, this piece is only one part of a larger work. It represents a good entry point into Tod Dockstader's organized sounds. But for a fuller immersion, try listening to all six parts of his *Water Music* (about 18 minutes) or his 1966 epic *Quatermass* (about 45 minutes).
7. **Karlheinz Stockhausen, 'Gesang der Jünglinge' (1956) [13:05]**
   This was the first major work to combine the concrete sounds of Paris with the artificial tones of Cologne. It also represents a vital touching point between the avant-garde and popular music through its influence on The Beatles and other key artists of the 1960s.

8. **The Beatles, 'Revolution 9' (1968) [8:22]**
The only reason most people have heard of musique concrète is because of this (in)famous track. It's undoubtedly the most widely heard artefact of the genre, with millions of physical sales as part of The Beatles' *White Album*, and millions of streams in the digital era.
9. **Bernard Parmegiani, 'Du pop à l'âne' (1969) [10:08]**
By 1969, there had been countless examples of the avant-garde influencing pop music. But this track shows how that influence flowed in both directions. Bernard Parmegiani incorporates extracts from Pink Floyd, The Doors and other rock artists into this acousmatic piece. He took a similar approach with another 1969 track, 'Pop'eclectic'.
10. **Beatriz Ferreyra, 'Echos' (1978, released 2020) [8:33]**
During her time at the GRM, Beatriz Ferreyra's work only had limited releases. But decades later, her compositions became widely available on a series of albums, which combined new works with archival content. This track attracted most attention, drawing widespread acclaim from critics.